go getter 1

CB130950

Student's Book

Sandy Zervas • Catherine Bright

Contents

Grammar/Communication video · Grammar animation · Culture video

Contents

0 Get started!

How do you spell that?

I can say and spell my name and surname.

In this unit

- *I'm … / My name is …*
- *This is …*
- *My/your*
- The alphabet
- Spelling words/names
- Numbers
- Colours
- In my bag
- Classroom objects
- Classroom language

0.1 Intro video

Hello!

1 1 1.2 **Watch or listen and read. Who is not from the UK?**

2 Look at the photos and read. Complete the children's hobbies.

1 Jen *making cupcakes*
2 Alex computers and ________
3 Lian all ________
4 Lucas ________ and Maths

3 Game! Stand in a line. Ask and answer.

A: *Hi, I'm Mario. What's your name?*
B: *I'm Isabella. Hi, I'm Isabella. What's your name?*
C: *My name's David. …*

4 1.3 1.4 Listen and do the Alphabet Rap.

, , , D,

E, F, G,

Say the alphabet, say it with me!

H, I, J, K, L, M, N, O, P,

 is funny as you can see.

R, S, T, U and V

four more letters and we're free.

W, X, Y and – Shh …

 is sleepy, so are we!

5 Complete the words with the letters in the box. Say the letters.

t h ~~g~~ x l s

1 *g*irl

2 bo_

3 _andwich

4 _able

5 _ion

6 fis_

6 1.5 Listen and tick (✔) the letters you hear.

1 A ☑ E ☑ I ☐
2 G ☐ J ☐ C ☐
3 W ☐ U ☐ Y ☐
4 B ☐ D ☐ P ☐
5 M ☐ N ☐ F ☐
6 I ☐ J ☐ Y ☐

7 Work in pairs. Say the alphabet. Stop when the teacher tells you. Your partner says what comes next.

A, B, C, D, … *Stop!* *E!*

LOOK! LL = double L

8 1.6 Listen to the surnames. Complete the missing letters. Check with your partner.

1 *N* E *W* M *A* N
2 _ R _ I _
3 _ A _ E _ _ _ _ _
4 _ _ G _ _ N _

9 Work in pairs. Ask for your partner's surname. Write it down.

A: *What's your surname?*
B: *Brown.*
A: *How do you spell that?*
B: *B-R-O-W-N.*

Fun Spot

10 Have a class spelling competition.

Apple. A-double P-L-E. Apple.

0.2 Numbers and colours

I can say numbers 0–100 and name basic colours.

Meet Dug and Kit

This is Dug. Dug is also Superdug. Superdug is a superhero.

This is Kit. Kit is very clever. She is Dug's best friend.

1 🔊 **1.7 Listen and read. Look at the picture. Then circle the correct answer.**

Dug / Kit is a superhero.

2 🔊 **1.8 Listen and repeat.**

Vocabulary Numbers 1–20

1 one	11 eleven
2 two	12 twelve
3 three	13 thirteen
4 four	14 fourteen
5 five	15 fifteen
6 six	16 sixteen
7 seven	17 seventeen
8 eight	18 eighteen
9 nine	19 nineteen
10 ten	20 twenty

3 Complete the numbers.

1 o *n* e	**7** _ e _ e _
2 _ w _	**8** e i _ _ t
3 t _ r _ _	**9** _ i n _
4 _ o _ r	**10** t _ _
5 f _ _ e	**11** _ l e _ _ n
6 _ i _	**12** t _ e _ v _

4 Write the answers in words.

1 six + six = *twelve*
2 eighteen – three = ________
3 two + eleven = ________
4 twenty – nine = ________
5 seventeen – three = ________
6 two + seven = ________
7 five + two = ________
8 sixteen – twelve = ________

5 1.9 Listen and repeat.

Vocabulary Numbers 10–100

10 ten	60 sixty
20 twenty	70 seventy
30 thirty	80 eighty
40 forty	90 ninety
50 fifty	100 a hundred

6 Circle the correct number.

1 forty	*14 / 40*	4 eighty	*18 / 80*
2 fifteen	*15 / 50*	5 twenty	*12 / 20*
3 thirteen	*13 / 30*	6 sixteen	*16 / 60*

7 1.10 Listen and write the number you hear.

a *20* d ____ g ____
b ____ e ____ h ____
c ____ f ____

8 1.11 Listen and repeat.

Vocabulary Colours

black blue brown green grey
orange pink purple red
white yellow

9 Look at Exercise 3. Write numbers which are this colour. There are two numbers for one of the colours.

red	*9*	green	____	pink	____
grey	____	white	____	black	____
blue	____	purple	____	brown	____
orange	____	yellow	____		

10 Game! Student A: Listen to Student B and guess! Then swap roles.

A: *What's your favourite colour?*
B: *Not pink, not brown, not white, not yellow, not green, not red, not blue, not grey, not black, not orange.*
A: *It's purple!*

11 Look at the picture below. Match 1–8 to a–h.

1 The elephants are	a blue.
2 The flowers are	b black and white.
3 The zebras are	c red.
4 The sky is	d grey.
5 The oranges are	e green.
6 The lemons are	f pink.
7 The trees are	g orange.
8 The flamingoes are	h yellow.

12 Game! Finish the sentences.

A: *The elephants are …*
B: *… green.*
C: *No! They're grey. The flowers are …*
D: *Red!*
E: *Yes! The zebras are …*

0.3 In the classroom

I can talk about classroom objects and understand classroom instructions.

1 1.12 **Listen and repeat. Name the objects in Jen's school bag.**

Vocabulary In my bag

book coloured pencil notebook pen pencil pencil case pencil sharpener rubber ruler sandwich scissors

LOOK! a book, a pencil
an apple, an umbrella

2 Write *a* or *an* before the words.

1 _a_ notebook
2 _an_ apple
3 ___ pencil
4 ___ egg
5 ___ ruler
6 ___ elephant
7 ___ book
8 ___ orange

LOOK!

a pencil	six pencils
an orange	two oranges
a box	four boxes
a sandwich	two sandwiches

3 Look at the picture. How many of these objects can you see in Jen's bag?

1 notebook? _Three notebooks._
2 pencil sharpener? ________
3 rubber? ________
4 sandwich? ________
5 coloured pencil? ________
6 pencil case? ________

4 1.13 **Listen and repeat. Check the meaning of these words in a dictionary.**

Vocabulary Classroom objects

bin board chair clock desk

5 Find the objects in the Vocabulary box in your classroom and point to them. How many are there?

LOOK! It's a pencil.
They're pencils.

6 **Work in pairs. Guess what these objects are. Then go to page 106 and check.**

1 It's a ____________

2 They're ________

3 ____________

4 ____________

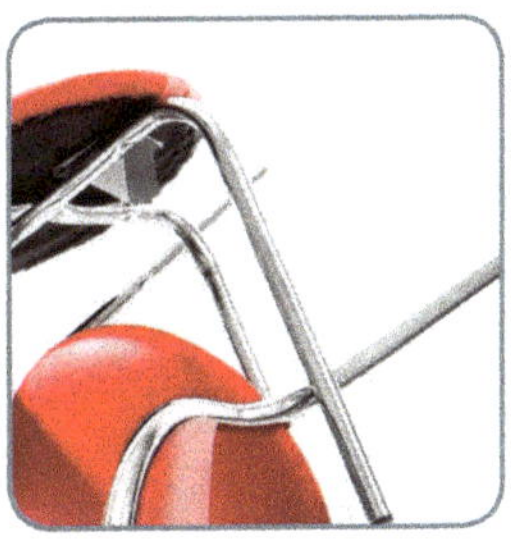

5 ____________

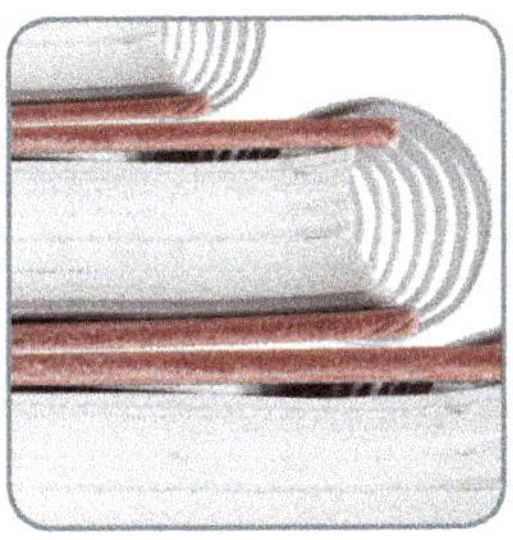

6 ____________

7 1.14 **Listen and repeat.**

Communication **Classroom language**

Close your books.	Work in pairs.
Listen (*to the story*).	Write (*your name*).
Look (*at the photo*).	
Open your books.	Can you help me?
Read (*the text*).	Can you repeat (that)?
Sit down.	I'm ready.
Stand up.	What's *kredka* in English?

8 **Read the expressions in the Communication box again. Who usually says them: Teacher or Student?**

LOOK!

Can you help me, please?
Stand up, please!

9 1.15 **Match 1–5 to a–e. Listen and check. Act out the dialogues in pairs.**

1 [e] Can you repeat that, please?
2 [ ] Can you help me, Miss?
3 [ ] How do we say *elefante* in English?
4 [ ] I'm ready!
5 [ ] What does *amazing* mean?

a We say *elephant*.
b Good. Class, are you ready too?
c It means *really good*.
d Yes, Maria. How can I help you?
e Yes, Tomas. Giraffe. Giraffe. OK?

Fun Spot

10 **Game! Be a teacher. Tell other students what to do. Use the expressions in the Communication box.**

1 Family and friends

Vocabulary I can talk about people in a family.

In this unit

Vocabulary
- Family
- Countries and nationalities
- Places

Grammar
- possessive *'s*
- *to be* affirmative
- possessive adjectives
- *to be* negative

2–3

1.2 Grammar video

4

1.2 Grammar animation

5

1.3 Grammar animation

6

1.4 Communication video

7

BBC Culture video

I know that!

1 Read these words. What do they mean?

brother dad grandad granny mum sister

2 1.16 Listen and repeat. Find the people in Mark's family pyramid on page 10. Use the colours to help you.

Vocabulary Family

mother mum father dad parents
grandfather grandad grandmother granny
son daughter brother sister
aunt uncle cousin

3 Complete the family words. Use the Vocabulary box to help you.

He	She
father	*mother*
______	grandmother
son	______
______	sister
uncle	______
______	cousin

4 Match 1–4 to a–d.

1 father — b
2 grandmother
3 mother
4 grandfather

a grandad
b dad
c granny
d mum

LOOK!
Paul = Mark's father
Lucy = Rose's daughter

5 Look at the family pyramid on page 10 and write the names.

1 Mark's grandfather *John*
2 Mark's sister ______
3 Mark's aunt ______
4 Mark's brother ______
5 Mark's cousins ______ ______
6 Mark's grandmother ______
7 Mark's uncle ______
8 Mark's parents ______ ______

6 Look at the family pyramid again. Complete the sentences. Use the names in the box.

~~Mark's~~ Julia's Rose's Tom's Paul's Peter's

1 Peter is *Mark's* uncle.
2 Julia is ______ sister.
3 David is ______ son.
4 Anna is ______ daughter.
5 John and Agatha are ______ parents.
6 Lucy is ______ cousin.

7 1.17 Listen and circle T (true) or F (false). Then listen again and check your answers.

1 T / (F)

2 T / F

3 T / F

4 T / F

5 T / F

6 T / F

I remember that!

8 Draw your family pyramid. Write the names of the people from your family.

1.2 Grammar

I can use the affirmative form of the verb *to be* and *my*, *your*, *his*, *her*.

It's Granny's birthday!

Today is Sophie's birthday. She is seventy years old. Sophie is Jen and Alex's grandmother. They are at her house.

1

Sophie: I'm so happy you're here.

2

Alex: It's aunt Megan!
Megan: Hello, Alex! Hold this, please! Be careful! It's Granny's birthday cake
Alex: It's OK. I've got it!

3

Megan: Happy birthday, Mum! Here's your present.
Sophie: Thank you, my darling. Where's your son?
Megan: Jason is in Spain with his class. They're on a school trip. Here's a card from him.
Sophie: Oh, it's a lovely card!
Dad: Hello, sister!

4

Dad: We're ready for the cake
Mum: Oh, no!

1 2 1.18 **Watch or listen and read. Answer the questions.**

1 How old is Jen and Alex's granny today?
2 Who is Jason?

2 Read the sentences. Circle T (true) or F (false). Correct the false sentences.

1 Granny's name is Sophie. (T) / F
2 They are at Jen and Alex's house. T / F
3 There's a present for Granny in the box. T / F
4 Jason is at home. T / F
5 Dad is Aunt Megan's brother. T / F

3 1.19 **Listen and repeat. Find these expressions in the story.**

Say it!

Hold this, please! Be careful! I've got it!

4 **Guess!** **Jen and Alex's mum says 'Oh, no!' Why? Have a class vote. Choose a, b or c.**

a The cake is a mess. **b** It's not Granny's cake.
c There's a mouse in the box.

5 3 1.20 **Now watch or listen and check.**

Grammar *to be affirmative*

Long form	Short form
I **am** ten.	I'**m** ten.
You **are** ten.	You'**re** ten.
He/She/It **is** ten.	He/She/It'**s** ten.
We **are** ten.	We'**re** ten.
You **are** ten.	You'**re** ten.
They **are** ten.	They'**re** ten.

4 Get Grammar!

6 **Find the sentences in the story. Write the missing word.**

1 They *are* at her house.
2 'I ______ so happy!'
3 'You ______ here!'
4 'It ______ Granny's birthday cake.'
5 'Jason ______ in Spain.'
6 'We ______ ready for the cake!'

7 **Circle the correct answer.**

1 You *(are)* / *is* ready.
2 I *is* / *am* here.
3 We *am* / *are* happy!
4 Jason *is* / *am* Jen's cousin.
5 It *are* / *is* a present for you.
6 Jen and Alex *is* / *are* at their Granny's house.

8 **Rewrite sentences 1, 2, 3 and 5 in Exercise 7 using short forms of the verb *to be*.**

1 *You're ready.*

LOOK!

I	→ my	It's **my** birthday. **I**'m ten!
you	→ your	It's **your** birthday. **You**'re eleven!
he	→ his	It's **his** birthday. **He**'s twelve.
she	→ her	It's **her** birthday. **She**'s nine.

9 **Complete with *my, your, his* or *her*.**

1 **Alex:** 'Granny, here's *your* birthday card!'
2 **Dad:** 'It's my mother's birthday. We are at ______ house.'
3 **Sophie:** 'I'm very happy! ______ family is here!'
4 **Megan:** 'Jason is in Spain with ______ class.'
5 **Alex:** '______ birthday cake is in this box, Granny.'

10 1.21 **How old are they? Follow the lines and complete the sentences. Then listen and check.**

1 **Lucas:** 'I *'m* *eleven*.' — 10
2 **Lian:** 'Alex and I ______ ______.' — 16
3 **Lucas:** 'My brother ______ ______.' — 11
4 **Lian to Jen:** 'You ______ ______, right?' — 12

11 **Read and complete with *am, are* or *is*.**

My name [1] *is* Lian and I [2] ______ twelve years old. Alex and I [3] ______ best friends and classmates. His sister, Jen, [4] ______ ten years old. We [5] ______ friends too.

12 **Look at Exercise 11. Write about you and your friends.**

My name's … and I …

Fun Spot

13 **Read the poem. Make changes to talk about a friend or a classmate.**

I'm ten today.
Hip, hip, hooray!
Let's have a break.
And eat **my** cake!

Ola's eleven today. …

1.3 Grammar

I can talk about countries and nationalities and use the negative form of the verb *to be*.

The Terrific Two Dug's family album

1 **Look at the cartoon. How many types of dogs can you see?**

2 1.22 **Listen and read. What nationality is Uncle Roberto?**

3 **Read the sentences. Circle T (true) or F (false).**

1 Uncle Roberto is a superhero. (T)/ F
2 Aunt Gigi is French. T / F
3 Dug's parents are superheroes. T / F
4 Dug is happy in the photo. T / F
5 Dug's mum is British. T / F

Grammar *to be* negative

Long form	Short form
I **am not** Spanish.	I**'m not** Spanish.
You **are not** Spanish.	You **aren't** Spanish.
He/She/It **is not** Spanish.	He/She/It **isn't** Spanish.
We **are not** Spanish.	We **aren't** Spanish.
You **are not** Spanish.	You **aren't** Spanish.
They **are not** Spanish.	They **aren't** Spanish.

5 **Get Grammar!**

4 **In your notebook, write negative sentences. Use the long form of the verb *to be*.**

1 Dug is French. *Dug is not French.*
2 Kit is a dog.
3 Dug's parents are superheroes.
4 Dug: 'I am happy.'
5 Kit: 'You are in the photo, Dug'.
6 Dug is hungry.

5 **Rewrite the sentences in Exercise 4 in your notebook. Use the short form of the verb *to be*.**

1 *Dug isn't French.*

6 1.23 **Look, listen and repeat.**

Vocabulary
Countries and nationalities

- the UK / British
- Spain / Spanish
- Poland / Polish
- the USA / American
- Italy / Italian
- France / French
- China / Chinese

7 **Look at the flags. Complete the sentences about Dug's family with *is* or *isn't*. Correct the false sentences.**

1 Aunt Teresa *isn't* Spanish. *She is Polish.*
2 Grandad Umberto _____ Chinese.
3 Cousin Lulu _____ French.
4 Cousin Chen _____ British.
5 Granny Flossie _____ American.

8 **In your notebook, write sentences about Kit's friends and family.**

1 Italy ✗ the UK ✓

2 Spain ✗ the UK ✓

3 France ✗ the UK ✓

4 the USA ✗ China ✓

Fun Spot

9 **Choose your nationality and play Three Guesses game.**

A: *You're Spanish!*
B: *No, I'm not Spanish.*
A: *You're British!*
B: *No, I'm not British.*
A: *You're Italian!*
B: *Yes, I'm Italian.*

1.4 Communication I can make introductions.

Nice to meet you!

Jen: Hi, Mum!
Mum: Hi, kids!
Jen: Mum, this is Lucas. He's our new neighbour. Lucas, this is my mum.
Mum: Hello, Lucas. Nice to meet you.
Lucas: Nice to meet you too, Mrs Newman.
Mum: Jen, your bag!
Jen: Sorry, Mum. Let's go, Lucas.

1 6 1.24 **Watch or listen and read. What's Jen's family name?**

2 1.25 **Listen and repeat.**

Communication Introductions

A: *Mum*, this is *Lucas*.
He is *my friend/classmate*.
Lucas, this is *my mum*.
B: Hello, *Lucas*. Nice to meet you.
C: Nice to meet you too.

3 1.26 **Put the dialogue in the correct order. Then listen and check.**

1 *b* 2 ☐ 3 ☐ 4 ☐

a **Desi:** Nice to meet you too, Lisa.
b **Adam:** Lisa, this is Desi. He's my best friend.
c **Lisa:** Hello, Desi. Nice to meet you.
d **Adam:** Desi, this is my cousin, Lisa.

4 **In groups of three, act out the dialogue in Exercise 3.**

5 **Exam Spot** **Circle the best answer.**

1 A: Hello, I'm George.
B: a Very well, thanks. b I've got it. c Nice to meet you, George.
2 A: Mum, this is Sam.
B: a He's my classmate. b Hello, Sam. c Hold this, please.
3 A: Kate, this is my sister, Lisa.
B: a Be careful! b Hi, Lisa. Nice to meet you. c She's my friend.

Fun Spot

6 **Write the names of three famous people. Then introduce them to your friends!**

Famous pop star ________
Famous film star ________
Famous sports person ________

My family album

I'm Alice! I'm twelve.
I'm from London in the UK.

This is my family album.

A

This is my favourite photo.

I'm four and my sister, Isabel, is six! We aren't at home in this photo. We're at my granny's house in London. Granny is Dad's mum. She's fun!

B

My cousin Tommy, Isabel and I are in this photo.

We're in the park near my house. I'm nine, Tommy's ten and Isabel's eleven.

C

And this is my family: Mum, Dad, Isabel and I.

I'm eleven and Isabel's thirteen. We're on holiday in France. My mum and my Aunt Jackie (Mum's sister) are French. Vincent's in the photo too. He's Aunt Jackie's dog. He's great.

1 1.27 **Read and listen to Alice's blog. Find Alice in photos A, B and C.**

2 **Complete the sentences about the text with one word.**

1 Isabel is Alice's *sister* .
2 Alice's mum and aunt are ________ .
3 Vincent is ________ Jackie's dog.
4 Tommy is Isabel's ________ .
5 Granny is ________'s mum.

3 **Exam Spot** **Read the sentences. Circle T (true) or F (false).**

1 Alice is eleven in Photo C. (T) / F
2 They're on holiday in France in Photo A. T / F
3 They are in the park in Photo B. T / F
4 Tommy is eleven in Photo B. T / F
5 Photo A is Alice's favourite. T / F

4 1.28 **Listen and repeat.**

Vocabulary Places

at home at school at a party
in the garden in the park on holiday

5 **Look at the pictures and write the places.**

a 
in the park

b 
____

c 
____

d 
____

e 
____

f 
____

6 1.29 **Listen and match conversations 1–4 to places a–f in Exercise 5. There are two extra places.**

1 *d* 2 ☐ 3 ☐ 4 ☐

7 **Work in pairs. Student A: Go to page 106. Student B: Go to page 108.**

1.6 Listening and Writing

I can understand and write short texts about best friends.

1 Look at the website. What is the radio show about?

2 1.30 Listen to the radio show. Match callers 1–3 to photos of their best friends A–C.

1 Tom ☐ 2 Maria ☐ 3 Juan ☐

A

B

C

3 Exam Spot 1.30 Read the questions. Listen again. Write a number or a country.

1 How old is Monica? *11*
2 Where is Monica now? ______
3 How old is Jack? ______
4 Where are Giorgia and Toni from? ______

4 Who's your best friend? Tell the class.

5 Read Jen's blog and complete the table.

Me and my best friend

My name's Jen. I'm ten and I'm from the UK. I'm British. My best friend is my neighbour, Lucas. He's eleven. Lucas and his family are from Spain. They're Spanish.

	Name	Age	Nationality	Country
Me	*Jen*			*the UK*
My best friend			*Spanish*	

Writing Capital letters

Use a capital letter for names of people, countries and nationalities.
Use a capital letter for the pronoun *I* and at the beginning of every sentence too.

My best friend is Jack. I'm from France.
Giorgia and Toni are Italian.

6 Find and circle capital letters in Jen's blog in Exercise 5.

7 Writing Time Write about you and your best friend.

Find ideas
Find a photo of you and your best friend. Make notes.

Draft
Write about your name, age, country and nationality.
My name's … I'm (ten/eleven/twelve …)
I'm from …
Write the same about your best friend.

Check and write
Check all the capital letters and write the final version of your text.

Vocabulary

1 Complete the family words. What seven other family words do you know?

1 g *r* a n d *a* d	4 a _ _ t	7 c o _ _ i n
2 g r _ n _ y	5 m _ m	8 s _ s t _ r
3 u n _ _ e	6 d _ d	9 b _ _ t _ e r

2 Circle the odd one out.

	a	b	c
1	*(Chinese)*	Spain	the UK
2	the USA	Italian	the UK
3	France	Poland	American
4	Spanish	British	China
5	French	the USA	Polish

3 Look at the pictures. Circle a, b or c.

1 
a in the park
b at school
c in the garden

2 
a at home
b on holiday
c at a party

3 
a on holiday
b at home
c in the garden

Pronunciation

4 1.31 Listen and repeat: /v/ or /b/?

Viv's best friends,
Vincent and Brad,
are a bad brown dog
and a very big cat!

Grammar

5 Write sentences with possessive 's.

1 Luke / cake — It's *Luke's cake* .
2 Granny / birthday — It's ________ .
3 Megan / son — Jason is ________ .
4 Dad / sister — Megan is ________ .

6 Read and complete Maria's profile with *am*, *are* or *is*.

My name's Maria.

I [1]*am* thirteen. I [2]_____ from the USA. My best friend [3]_____ Isabel. Her family [4]_____ English. We [5]_____ classmates. Her two brothers [6]_____ my friends too.

7 Match 1–5 to a–e.

1 [c] Jane's best
2 [ ] Your brother is
3 [ ] It's my
4 [ ] That isn't
5 [ ] His cousin

a your schoolbag.
b George is eleven.
c friend is her neighbour.
d in my class.
e birthday today!

8 Write negative sentences. Which sentences are true for you? Tell your partner.

1 I'm fifteen. / *I'm not fifteen* .
2 My best friend is my cat. / ________ .
3 My brother's name is Ben. / ________ .
4 We're at home. / ________ .
5 It's my birthday. / ________ .
6 My neighbours are my classmates. / ________ .

Communication

9 Complete the dialogue with the words in the box. Then act out the dialogue in groups of three.

Nice ~~this~~ meet this

Jamie: Mum, [1]*this* is my friend, David.
David, [2]_____ is my mum.
David: Hello, Mrs Smith. [3]_____ to meet you.
Mum: Nice to [4]_____ you too, David.

Check yourself!

- I can talk about people in a family. [ ]
- I can talk about countries and nationalities. [ ]
- I can use possessive 's. [ ]
- I can use the affirmative and negative forms of the verb *to be*. [ ]
- I can use possessive adjectives *my*, *your*, *his*, *her*. [ ]
- I can make introductions. [ ]

Get Culture!

English around the world

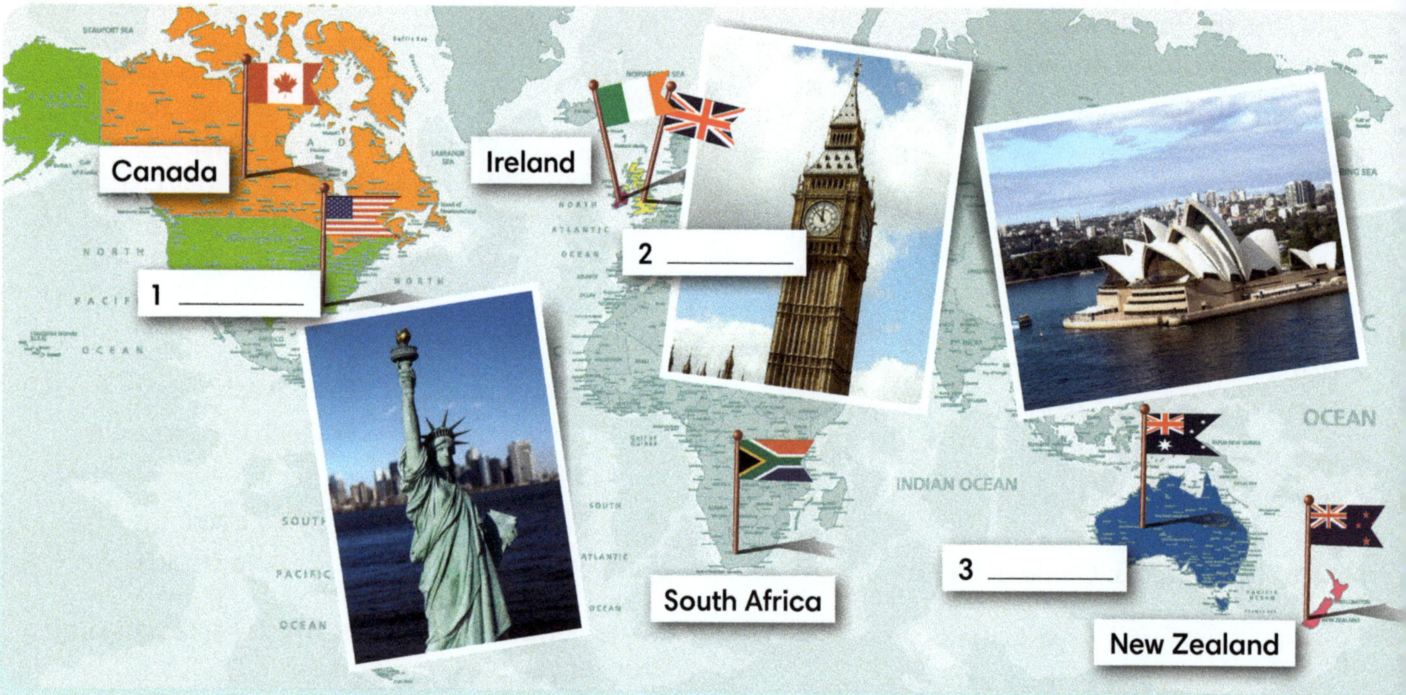

1 **Look at the map. Label countries 1–3 with the words in the box.**

the UK	the USA	Australia

2 🔊 **1.32 People in the UK, the USA and Australia speak the same language. What language is it? Read, listen and check.**

Who speaks English?

The UK The capital city of the United Kingdom, or UK, is London. The UK is four different countries: England, Wales, Scotland and Northern Ireland. There are about 65 million people in the UK and English is the official language.

The USA The USA is short for the United States of America. The capital of the USA is Washington. There are 324 million people in the USA. They speak English but about 37 million people speak Spanish too.

Australia 24 million people live in Australia. Its capital city is Canberra and Sydney is its biggest city. Most people speak English in Australia. Here's an interesting fact: when it's winter in the UK and the USA, it is summer in Australia.

3 **Look at the map and read the text again. Read tasks 1–6 and follow the instructions.**

1 Circle the Australian flag.
a  b  c 

2 Complete the sentence.
Scotland is in ______ .

3 Number the countries from 1 to 3 (very big, big, small number of people).
☐ The UK ☐ The USA ☐ Australia

4 Write T (true) or F (false).
Christmas is in the summer in Australia. ____

5 Circle the correct answer.
Sydney is in *Australia / the USA*.

6 Complete the sentence.
Many people speak Spanish in ______ .

4 🔊 **1.33 Listen and match 1–4 to a–d.**

1 [c]	Erin	a is from the USA.
2 ☐	Peter	b is from Australia.
3 ☐	Ollie	c is from the UK.
4 ☐	Mary	d is from London, UK.

5 **Game! Say three facts about the UK, the USA or Australia for your partner to guess the country.**

A: *The capital city is Canberra.*
B: *It's Australia!*

This is the UK

A 7 **Watch the video and answer the presenter's questions. Who is Harry?**

B 7 **Watch the video again. Circle the correct answer a, b or c.**

1 The UK is: The United Kingdom of Great Britain and …
   a Scotland. b Wales. c Northern Ireland.
2 People from the UK are …
   a British. b English. c American.
3 There are … million people in London.
   a 4 b 9 c 64
4 Queen Elizabeth is Prince William's
   a grandson. b grandmother. c aunt.

C Discuss in class. What new things did you learn from the video? Would you like to visit the UK? Why/Why not?

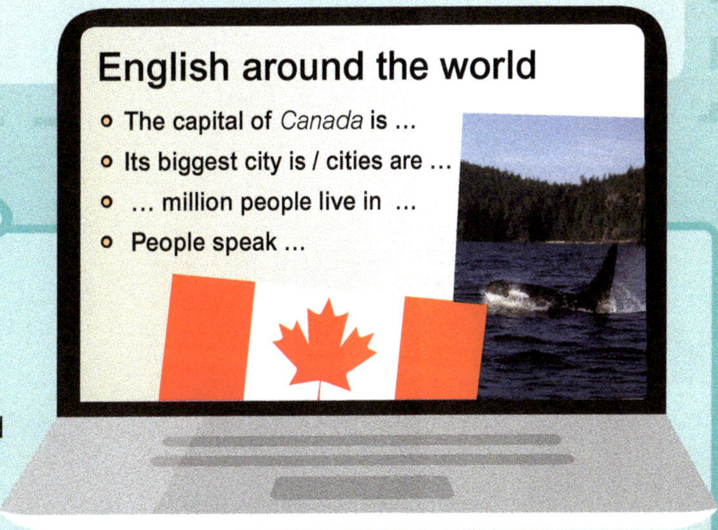

PROJECT

- **Work in four groups. Prepare a digital presentation about one of these countries.**

  The Republic of Ireland | New Zealand
  The Republic of South Africa | Canada

- **Write information about the country. Use these questions to help you.**

  How many people live in this country?
  What is the capital city? What are other big cities?
  What language(s) do people speak there?

- **Add a map of the country, its flag and photos of important and/or interesting places.**
- **Share your presentation with the class.**

2 My things

Vocabulary I can talk about clothes.

In this unit

Vocabulary
- Clothes
- Adjectives
- My things

Grammar
- *this, that, these, those*
- *too big/small*
- *to be* questions and short answers

I know that!

1 Find these clothes in the picture. Which are you wearing today?

coat   jeans   shoes   skirt   T-shirt   trousers

8-9

2.2 Grammar video

10

2.2 Grammar animation

11

2.3 Grammar animation

12

2.4 Communication video

2 🔊 1.34 **Listen and repeat. Find the clothes in the picture on page 22.**

Vocabulary Clothes

boots cap coat dress hoodie jacket jeans jumper shirt shoes skirt T-shirt top tracksuit trainers trousers

3 🔊 1.35 **Listen and circle the word you hear.**

1 (T-shirt) / shirt
2 jacket / jumper
3 trainers / trousers
4 shoes / skirt
5 cap / coat
6 boots / hoodie

LOOK!
The T-shirt **is** blue.
The shoes **are** brown.
The jeans **are** blue.

4 Complete the table with the words in the Vocabulary box.

is	are
T-shirt, ______, ______, ______, ______, ______, ______, ______, ______, ______, ______	*shoes,* ______, ______
	jeans, ______

5 Complete the sentences with *is* or *are*. Then look at the picture on page 22. Tick (✔) for *yes* or put a cross (✘) for *no*.

1 [✘] The tracksuit *is* black.
2 [ ] The dress ______ yellow.
3 [ ] The trainers ______ red.
4 [ ] The hoodie ______ grey.
5 [ ] The boots ______ brown.
6 [ ] The trousers ______ green.

6 Look at your clothes and tell a partner.

My jeans are blue, my T-shirt is green and white and my trainers are red.

7 Choose a student from your class and name his or her clothes. Ask your partner to guess.

A: *White T-shirt, blue skirt.*
B: *It's Natasha!*

8 Adam and Adele are in the sports centre. Are their clothes OK? Complete the list. Tick (✔) for *yes* or put a cross (✘) for *no*.

Adam: 1 *T-shirt* [✔] 2 *jacket* [✘]
3 ______ [ ] 4 ______ [ ]
Adele: 5 ______ [ ] 6 ______ [ ]
7 ______ [ ] 8 ______ [ ]

9 Dress Adam and Adele for a party. Write two lists of clothes. Then compare in pairs.

Adam: *white T-shirt, …*
Adele: *pink dress, …*

I remember that!

10 Make lists of clothes you wear at school and at the weekend.

at school	at the weekend

2.2 Grammar

I can use *this, that, these, those* and adjectives.

That's my T-shirt!

1

Mum: Jen, put these clothes away, please.
Jen: OK, Mum.
Oh, hi! What's up?
What? No!

Ten minutes later …

2

Jen: Bye, Holly! … Hang on, what are these? These aren't my jeans. They're too long! These are Mum's jeans! Yep, this top is Mum's too!

3

Mum: Jen, these are your jeans. They're too small for me!
Jen: Oops! Sorry, Mum!
Mum: And that's my top over there.
Jen: Yes, it is. Here you are!

4

Alex: Jen? … Jen, where's my new T-shirt?
Jen: It's over there with your old T-shirts!
Alex: No, those are Dad's T-shirts!
Jen: Oh, then your T-shirt is …

1 8 1.36 **Watch or listen and read. Are the clothes in the right place?**

2 Look at the photos and read the story again. Whose clothes are they? Circle the correct answer.

1 **Photo 2** The jeans are *Jen's* / *Mum's*.
2 **Photo 3** The jeans are *Jen's* / *Mum's*.
3 **Photo 3** The top is *Jen's* / *Mum's*.
4 **Photo 4** The T-shirts are *Dad's* / *Alex's*.

3 1.37 **Listen and repeat. Find these expressions in the story.**

Say it!

What's up? Hang on!
Here you are. Over there.

4 Guess! **Who's got Alex's new T-shirt? Have a class vote.**

a Mum **b** Dad **c** Jen

5 9 1.38 **Now watch or listen and check.**

Grammar *this, that, these, those*

▶ 10 **Get Grammar!**

This is Jen's top. This top is Jen's. 	That is Alex's T-shirt. That T-shirt is Alex's. 
These are Jen's trainers. These trainers are Jen's. 	Those are Alex's trainers. Those trainers are Alex's. 

6 Circle the correct answer.

1 *This* / *(These)* are your trainers.
2 *This* / *These* isn't Alex's shirt.
3 *This* / *These* shoes aren't Jen's.
4 *That* / *Those* T-shirts are Dad's.
5 *That* / *Those* is my coat.
6 *That* / *Those* boots are Mum's.

7 Complete with *this, that, these* or *those*.

1 → *That* is Alex's cap.
2 → ____ are Jen's trousers.
3 → ____ are Dad's jeans.
4 → ____ is Mum's top.
5 → ____ is Alex's jacket.

8 1.39 Listen and repeat.

Vocabulary Adjectives

big boring cool long new old
short small

9 Look at the words in the Vocabulary box. Write the opposites in your notebook.

1 *big – small*

10 In pairs, talk about the clothes. Use adjectives in the Vocabulary box and *this, that, these* or *those*.

A: *T-shirt 1.*
B: *This T-shirt is cool! T-shirt 2.*
A: *That T-shirt is boring. Trousers 2. …*

LOOK! Her boots are too big!
His shirt is too small!

11 What's wrong with her clothes? In your notebook, write sentences with *too*.

1 Her skirt / long
Her skirt is too long.
2 Her boots / old
3 Her top / small

12 Play a drawing dictation game. Use adjectives with *too*.

Draw a boy. His T-shirt is too small. …

The Terrific Two Dug's new suit

1 **Look at the cartoon. Where does Dug buy his superhero suits from?**

2 1.40 **Listen and read. What size is Dug's new suit?**

3 **Read the sentences. Circle T (true) or F (false).**

1 The dogs are OK. T / F
2 The girl is a superhero. T / F
3 Dug's new suit is in the box. T / F
4 Dug is cool in his new suit. T / F

Grammar *to be* questions and short answers

▶ 11 **Get Grammar!**

?	Short answers
Am I OK?	Yes, I am. / No, I'm not.
Are you OK?	Yes, you are. / No, you aren't.
Is he/she/it OK?	Yes, he/she/it is. / No, he/she/it isn't.
Are we OK?	Yes, you are. / No, you aren't.
Are you OK?	Yes, we are. / No, we aren't.
Are they OK?	Yes, they are. / No, they aren't.
What is it? It's my new suit.	

4 **Write questions. Who's asking the question? Write *boy*, *girl*, *Dug* or *Kit*.**

1 they OK Are ? *Are they OK?* *girl*
2 he a superhero Is ? ______ ______
3 you Are sure ? ______ ______
4 for me Is this box ? ______ ______
5 it What is ? ______ ______
6 cool I Am ? ______ ______

5 **Look at the cartoon. Answer the questions in Exercise 4.**

1 *Superdug: Yes, they are.*

6 **Complete the questions and the short answers.**

1 **Boy:** *Are* you a superhero?
Kit: No, I *'m not* .

2 **Kit:** ______ we best friends?
Dug: Yes, we ______ .

3 **Dug:** ______ my new suit cool?
Kit: No, it ______ .

4 **Kit:** ______ I clever?
Dug: Yes, you ______ .

5 **Girl:** ______ Superdug your brother?
Kit: No, he ______ .

6 **Kit:** ______ they your dogs?
Girl: Yes, they ______ .

7 1.41 **Listen to the questions and circle the correct answer.**

1 (Yes, it is.) / No, they aren't.
2 Yes, you are. / No, they aren't.
3 Yes, I am. / No, you aren't.
4 Yes, they are. / No, he isn't.
5 Yes, they are. / No, you aren't.
6 Yes, we are. / No, they aren't.

8 **Write questions in your notebook. Then ask the questions and give true answers in pairs.**

1 you / ten years old? *Are you ten years old?*
2 you / happy?
3 we / friends?
4 Superdug and Kit / cool?
5 you / clever?
6 I / a superhero?

A: *Are you ten years old?*
B: *Yes, I am. / No, I'm not.*

Fun Spot

9 1.42 1.43 **Go to page 107. Listen and chant Kit's Rap.**

2.4 Communication

I can ask for and give personal information.

What's your name?

Mr Wood: What's your name?
Lucas: Lucas Ortiz. That's O-R-T-I-Z.
Mr Wood: Good. And how old are you, Lucas?
Lucas: I'm eleven years old.
Mr Wood: Welcome to the school band.

Lian: Where are you from, Lucas?
Lucas: I'm from Madrid, Spain.
Lian: What's your favourite music?
Lucas: Good question. Rock, I think.
Lian: Who's your favourite singer?
Lucas: Erm … Ed Sheeran.
Lian: High five! He's my favourite too!

1 12 1.44 **Watch or listen and read. Where is Lucas from?**

2 1.45 **Listen and repeat.**

Communication
Asking for personal information

What's your name?
How old are you?
Where are you from?
What's your favourite *music/sport/film*?
Who's your favourite *actor/singer/sports person*?

3 1.46 **Listen to the dialogues. Circle the correct answer.**

1 *Star Wars.* / *Superman.*
2 Nick Carr. That's C-A-double R. / Carl Neal. That's N-E-A-L.
3 Warsaw, Poland. / Paris, France.
4 I'm twelve. / I'm thirteen.
5 Alicia Keys. / Taylor Swift.

4 Exam Spot **Complete the dialogues with questions in the Communication box.**

1 A: *What's your favourite music?*
B: Pop, I think.
2 A: ____________________?
B: I'm twelve years old.
3 A: ____________________?
B: My name's Fred Allen. That's A- double L-E-N.
4 A: ____________________?
B: Football.
5 A: ____________________?
B: I'm from Glasgow, Scotland.

Fun Spot

5 **In pairs, ask and answer questions in the Communication box. Give crazy answers!**

A: *What's your name?*
B: *My name's Queen Coco!*
A: *Where are you from?*
B: *I'm from Chocolateland!*

I can understand a text about a super backpack. **Reading** **2.5**

1 1.47 **Listen and repeat. Then label pictures 1–6 with the words in the Vocabulary box.**

Vocabulary My things

backpack games console laptop computer mobile phone mountain bike skateboard

1 *games console*

2 ______

3 ______

4 ______

5 ______

6 ______

2 1.48 **Read and listen to the article. Why is the backpack a super backpack?**

3 Read the sentences. Circle T (true) or F (false).

1 Jamie is from London in the UK. T / (F)
2 Super backpack is a jumper too. T / F
3 Super backpack is too small for a laptop computer. T / F
4 Fiona is Jamie's pet. T / F

4 Exam Spot Look at the picture in the text and answer the questions.

1 What colour is the super backpack? *It's red.*
2 What colour is the mountain bike? ______
3 Is the jacket red or blue? ______
4 Is the cat in the pocket big or small? ______

5 Work in groups. Invent a supergadget! Draw it and present it to the class.

It's a school bag. It's a skateboard too.

Jamie Cooper's 13.
He's from Liverpool in the UK.
Jamie's super backpack is our gadget of the week. Why? Read on.
CONGRATULATIONS, JAMIE!

Super backpack!

What's in the picture? Yes, that's right. It's a red backpack. It's a super backpack! It's very very cool.

Look again. This super backpack is also a mountain bike. It's small but it isn't too small. It's fantastic! And that's not all. Think about it. You're in the park with your friends. You're cold and your jumper is at home. No problem. This super backpack is a big jacket too.

What about your other things? Don't worry! Super backpack is just the right size for your laptop computer, your mobile phone, your new games and other favourites. There's even a pocket for a small pet like my cat Fiona. How cool is that?

2.6 Listening and Writing

I can understand and write short texts about favourite things.

1 Work in pairs. Name the clothes of the people in the picture in Exercise 2. What objects have they got?

2 Exam Spot 1.49 Look at the picture again. Listen and draw lines. There's one extra child.

3 Exam Spot 1.49 Listen again. Circle T (true) or F (false).

1 Sam's cap is too small. T / (F)
2 Janet is Monica's sister. T / F
3 Janet's skateboard is her favourite thing. T / F
4 Ben's backpack is blue. T / F
5 Monica's skirt is too short. T / F

4 What are your favourite things? Tell a friend.

5 Read Alex's blog post. Underline his favourite things.

What are my favourite things?

Today my post is about my favourite things. Are these my clothes, my computer or my phone? No! My number one favourite thing is my old blue mountain bike. I love my bike! My new comic book is number two. It's fantastic! What's number three? That's easy. My red and white trainers. They're really cool! Write a post and tell me about your favourite things!

Writing Punctuation

Remember to use punctuation marks!

What are your favourite things?
They're my backpack, my phone and my computer. They are cool!

6 Find and circle the punctuation marks in Alex's blog.

7 Writing Time Write about your favourite things.

Find ideas
Make a list of your favourite things.
Think of adjectives to describe them.

Draft
Write about your favourite things.
Give your text a title.
What are my favourite things?
My number one/two/three favourite thing is my … It's …

Check and write
Check your punctuation and write the final version of your text.

Vocabulary

1 Look at the pictures and complete the words. In pairs, say eight more clothes words.

1 boots
2 co_t
3 ju_pe_
4 ca_
5 tr_ine_s
6 je__s
7 sh__t
8 ja_k_t

2 Which picture a–c matches sentences 1–2? Describe the extra picture with a friend.

a

b

c

1 ☐ It's old but it isn't boring. It's green. It's cool!
2 ☐ It's new. It isn't small and it isn't big. It's red.

3 Find and circle four objects.

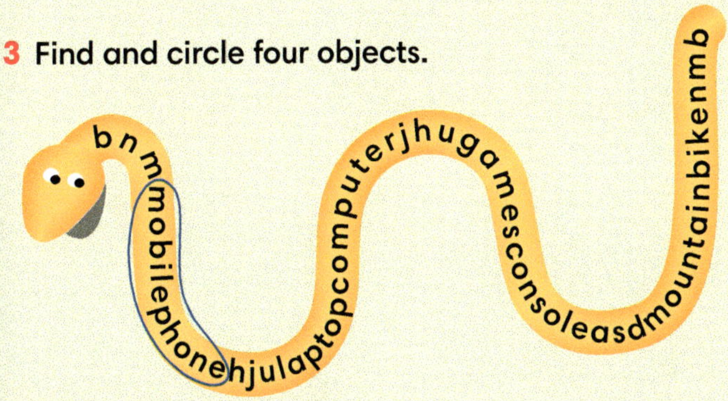

Pronunciation

4 1.50 Listen and repeat: /ð/ or /d/?

This cool hoodie is my brother Dan's.
That new dress is my mother Anne's.

Grammar

5 Look at the pictures in Exercise 1 again. In pairs, say sentences with *too*.

Maggie's coat is too big.

6 Match sentence halves 1–5 to a–e.

1 These are my favourite	a old and boring .
2 Those trousers	b her computer games.
3 Those aren't	c brown bike.
4 That phone is	d trainers.
5 This is my old	e are too long.

7 Write questions in your notebook. Answer *yes* (✔) or *no* (✘). Use short answers.

1 your / backpack / blue? ✔
Is your backpack blue? Yes, it is.
2 those / your / books ? ✘
3 he / at school? ✔
4 she / Italian? ✘
5 you / my best friend? ✔

Communication

**8 Write questions. Then work in pairs.
Student A: You are your favourite star.
Student B: Ask Student A questions 1–5.
Then swap roles.**

1 name What's your ?
What's your name?
2 How old you are ?
______
3 Where from you are ?
______
4 music favourite your What's ?
______
5 Who's favourite actor your ?
______

Check yourself! ☑

- I can talk about clothes. ☐
- I can use *this*, *that*, *these*, *those* and adjectives. ☐
- I can ask and answer questions with the verb *to be*. ☐
- I can ask for and give personal information. ☐

Reading and Writing

Cheryl is my new school friend. She's twelve. Her favourite colour is pink. Cheryl's pink mobile phone is her favourite thing. A lot of her clothes are pink too. Her pet dog, Rafs, isn't pink! He's grey and black.

Cheryl's family is very big. Sarah and Daniela are her sisters. Her brothers are Rob and Mick. Her dad is a guitarist in a band. Sometimes he's on TV shows! Her mum's a singer. She's very cool. Her granny and grandad are from Spain. They aren't boring. They are actors. They are in films! Are they all happy? Yes, they are!

1 **Work in pairs. Say what you can see in the photo.**

2 Exam Spot **Read the text. Circle the correct title.**

a Cheryl's new dog. b My new school friend.

3 **Read the sentences. Answer the questions.**

1 How old is Cheryl? *Cheryl is twelve.*
2 What's her favourite thing?
3 Is Cheryl's family small?
4 Who are Rob and Mick?
5 Is Cheryl's mum boring?
6 Where is her grandmother from?

4 Exam Spot **Look and read. Tick (✔) for *yes* or put a cross (✗) for *no*.**

1 ✔ 
This is a dog.

2 ☐ 
This is a skirt.

3 ☐ 
These are shoes.

4 ☐ 
These are skateboards.

5 ☐ 
This is a party.

6 ☐ 
These are jeans.

5 Exam Spot **Write 40–50 words about your friend. Use these questions to help you.**

1 What's his/her name?
2 How old is he/she?
3 What's his/her favourite colour?
4 What are his/her favourite things?
5 Where is his/her family from?

My good friend is … He/She is … years old. His/Her favourite colour is … His/Her favourite things are … His/Her family is from …

Listening

6 Exam Spot 1.51 **Read the questions. Listen and write a name or a number.**

1 What's the man's surname? *Smith*
2 What's the boy's name? ______
3 Who is the boy's best friend? ______
4 How old is the boy? ______
5 What's the number of the boy's house? ______

Communication

7 **Exam Spot** Look at the pictures. Match a–h to 1–6. There are two extra sentences.

a Nice to meet you.
b Who's your favourite actor?
c This is my mum.
d Caz, this is Jack.
e Hello Caz!
f He's my neighbour.
g What's your favourite music?
h Nice to meet you too, Mrs Smith.

8 **Exam Spot** Work in pairs. Ask and answer the questions.

1 What are your favourite weekend clothes?
2 What colour is your T-shirt/top today?
3 What's in your schoolbag today? (Don't look!)
4 What is your favourite place?

Exam Language Bank

Family
mother
mum
father
dad
parents
grandfather
grandad
grandmother
granny
son
daughter
brother
sister
aunt
uncle
cousin

Countries and nationalities
the UK / British
Spain / Spanish
Poland / Polish
the USA / American
Italy / Italian
France / French
China / Chinese

Places
at home
at school
at a party
in the garden
in the park
on holiday

Clothes
boots
cap
coat
dress
hoodie
jacket
jeans
jumper
shirt
shoes
skirt
T-shirt
top
tracksuit
trainers
trousers

Adjectives
big
boring
cool
long
new
old
short
small

My things
backpack
games console
laptop computer
mobile phone
mountain bike
skateboard

Introductions
Mum, this is *Lucas*.
He's my *friend/classmate*.
Lucas, this is *my mum*.
Nice to meet you.
Nice to meet you too.

Asking questions
What's your name?
How old are you?
Where are you from?
What's your favourite *music/sport/film*?
Who's your favourite *actor/singer/sportsperson*?

3 In the house

Vocabulary I can talk about my house.

In this unit

Vocabulary
- In the house
- Prepositions of place
- Household objects

Grammar
- *there is / there are* affirmative, negative and questions
- *a/an, any*

▶ 13–14

3.2 Grammar video

▶ 15

3.2 Grammar animation

▶ 16

3.3 Grammar animation

▶ 17

3.4 Communication video

▶ 18

BBC Culture video

I know that!

1 How many of these objects can you find in the photos?

bed chair desk door sofa table window

2 2.1 Listen and repeat. Find the items in the Vocabulary box in the photos on page 34.

Vocabulary In the house

Parts of the house

bathroom bedroom door floor garage garden kitchen living room wall window

Inside the house

armchair bath bed chair desk fridge sofa table wardrobe

3 Which part of the house are the photos from? Circle the correct answer.

1 living room / bedroom

2 bathroom / kitchen

3 garage / garden

4 bedroom / living room

5 living room / garden

6 floor / wall

4 2.2 Listen to the sounds. Where are you? Write in your notebook.

1 *In the living room.*

5 Complete the word. Read the sentence, look at the photos on page 34 and circle T (true) or F (false).

1 b e d
It's in the bathroom. T / F

2 f _ _ _ _ e
It's in the kitchen. T / F

3 a _ _ _ _ _ _ _ r
It's in the kitchen. T / F

4 w _ _ _ _ _ _ _ e
It's in the bedroom. T / F

5 t _ _ _ e
It's in the garden. T / F

6 b _ _ h
It's in the bathroom. T / F

7 c _ _ _ r
It's in the kitchen T / F

6 In your notebook, correct the false sentences in Exercise 5.

1 *The bed is in the bedroom.*

7 Look at the photos on page 34.
Student A: Say a sentence about an object inside the house.
Student B: Find the object in the photos. Is Student A's sentence true? Correct the false sentences.
Then swap roles.

A: *An armchair is in the bathroom.*
B: *No, it isn't. It's the living room!*

I remember that!

8 Draw where things are in your Crazy House. Then make lists and compare in pairs.

The kitchen: a sofa, …

I can use *there is* / *there are* and prepositions of place.

There's a phone on the sofa!

1 ▶13 🔊 2.3 **Watch or listen and read. What is Alex looking for? Circle the correct answer.**

a a book   b his phone   c a DVD

2 **Answer the questions.**

1 **Photo 1** Where are the three friends?
They're in the kitchen.
2 **Photo 2** Where are they now?
3 **Photo 2** Is it Jen's phone?
4 **Photo 3** Are they Alex's DVDs?
5 **Photo 4** What's wrong with the sweets?

3 🔊 2.4 **Listen and repeat. Find these expressions in the story.**

Say it!

Right there!   There it is!
Wait!   Yuk!

4 **Guess!** **Where is Alex's phone? Make a guess. Use *in*, *on* or *under*.**

5 ▶14 🔊 2.5 **Now watch or listen and check.**

Grammar
there is / there are affirmative

+ There's (There is) a phone on the sofa.

There are two DVDs behind the sofa.
There are some sweets under the sofa.

▶15 Get Grammar!

6 **Complete with *There is* or *There are*. Then look at the photos on page 36 and tick (✔) the true sentences.**

1 ☑ *There is* a fridge.
2 ☐ ________ one chair.
3 ☐ ________ a bed.
4 ☐ ________ four phones.
5 ☐ ________ two windows.
6 ☐ ________ a sofa.

7 **Look around. Say how many of them there are in your classroom.**

door window board desk
boys and girls teacher wall

There's one door. There are two windows.

8 🔊 2.6 **Look, listen and repeat.**

Vocabulary
Prepositions of place

behind | in | in front of
next to | on | under

9 **Look at the photos on page 36. Circle the correct preposition.**

1 **Photo 1** There are two phones *under* / (*on*) the kitchen table.
2 **Photo 1** Alex is *behind* / *in front of* the fridge.
3 **Photo 1** There is a carton of juice *in* / *next to* the fridge.
4 **Photo 1** Jen is *behind* / *next to* Alex.
5 **Photo 2** There are some books *under* / *on* the small table.

10 **Look at pictures A and B. Complete the sentences.**

1 *There's* a chair ...
A *in front of* the desk. B *on* the bed.
2 ________ a box ...
A ________ the desk. B ________ the door.
3 ________ a bag ...
A ________ the door. B ________ the box.
4 *There are* some books ...
A ________ the bag. B ________ the desk.
5 ________ some T-shirts ...
A ________ the bed. B ________ the bed.

Fun Spot

11 **Go to page 108 and play a drawing dictation game.**

The Terrific Two Dug and Coco

1 Look at the cartoon. How do Kit and Superdug talk when he is in the air? Circle the correct picture.

a  b  c 

2 2.7 Listen and read. Who is on the phone in Picture 1? Circle the correct answer.

a Kit's granny b Coco, the parrot

3 Complete the sentences with words from the cartoon.

1 *Kit's* granny's house is at 10 Paxton Stree
2 Granny's ________ is blue.
3 There are two big ________ in Granny's garde
4 There aren't any bad ________ in Granny's house.
5 There's only Granny and ________ in the hous

Grammar
there is / there are negative and questions

▶ 16 **Get Grammar!**

–	There isn't a red car.	There aren't any people.
?	Is there a red car? Yes, there is. / No, there isn't.	Are there any people? Yes, there are. / No, there aren't.

4 Circle the correct answer. Then look at the cartoon on page 38 and tick (✔) the true sentences.

1 ☑ *There isn't / (There aren't)* any people in Granny's garden.

2 ☐ *There isn't / There aren't* any cats in the story.

3 ☐ *There isn't / There aren't* a bike in Granny's garage.

4 ☐ *There isn't / There aren't* any dogs in Granny's garden.

5 ☐ *There isn't / There aren't* a phone in Granny's house.

6 ☐ *There isn't / There aren't* a desk in the living room.

LOOK!
There isn't **a** tree.
There aren't **any** trees.
Is there **a** tree?
Are there **any** trees?

5 Look at the cartoon again. What is missing? Choose from the box.

TV   photos   table   ~~window~~   doors

1 **Picture 1** Look behind Dug.
There isn't a window!

2 **Picture 2** Look at Granny's house.

3 **Picture 3** Look behind Granny.

4 **Picture 4** Look at the books.

5 **Picture 5** Look at the wall behind Coco.

6 Look at the picture. In your notebook, write Kit's questions and Dug's answers. Then ask and answer the questions in pairs.

1 a small house next to the big houses?
Kit: *Is there a small house next to the big houses?*
Dug: *Yes, there is.*

2 cars in front of the houses?

3 a dog under the tree?

4 people in the street?

5 chairs in the garden?

6 flowers next to the tree?

7 a cat behind the tree?

8 a parrot in the tree?

Fun Spot

7 Go to page 108 and play a memory game.

3.4 Communication

I can ask for something and ask where something is.

Where's the bathroom?

Jen: Hi! Here are your books.
Lucas: Thanks, Jen. Please, come in. Would you like a sandwich?
Jen: Yes, please. I'm really hungry.

Jen: This is yummy!
Lucas: Erm … Jen? There's ketchup on your T-shirt.
Jen: Oh, no! Where's the bathroom, please?
Lucas: It's upstairs. Let me show you.

Lucas: Is your T-shirt OK?
Jen: Not really. But I'd like another sandwich, please!

1 17 2.8 **Watch or listen and read. Whose house is it? Circle the correct answer.**

a Jen's   b Lian's   c Lucas's

2 2.9 **Listen and repeat.**

Communication Having a guest

A: Hello. Please, come in.
B: Thank you.
A: Would you like *a sandwich*?
B: Yes, please. / No, thank you.

A: Where's the *bathroom*, please?
B: It's *upstairs/downstairs*.
It's *next to* the *living room*.
Let me show you.

3 Match 1–3 to a–c. Then act out the dialogues in pairs.

1 ☐ Would you like a biscuit?
2 ☐ Where's the kitchen, please?
3 ☐ Where's my jacket, please?

a It's downstairs. Let me show you.
b It's on the chair, next to the sofa.
c Yes, please.

4 Exam Spot Circle the best answer.

1 A: Hello, Maria. Please, come in.
B: a Yes, please.   b Thank you.   c Let me show you.

2 A: Would you like an ice cream?
B: a Come in.   b It's downstairs.   c Yes, please.

3 A: Where's the bathroom?
B: a Please, come in.   b Let me show you.   c It's next to the bed.

5 Write dialogues. Then act them out in pairs.

1 A: Hi / come in   B: thank
Hi. Please, come in.   *Thank you.*
2 A: like / a cupcake?   B: no / thank
3 A: like / an apple?   B: yes
4 A: where / the bathroom?   B: It's / Let me show

Fun Spot

6 You have a guest from another planet. In pairs, write dialogues in English and in your guest's language. Then act them out in class.

A: *Hello, Xen! Please, come in.*
B: *Nabu midi rona, Tomi.*

1 2.10 **Listen and repeat. Then label pictures 1–6 with the words in the Vocabulary box.**

Vocabulary **Household objects**

carpet cushion lamp plant poster
television (TV)

1 *television*

2 ________

3 ________

4 ________

5 ________

6 ________

2 Which objects in Exercise 1 are in your classroom? Where are they? Tell a partner.

3 Exam Spot 2.11 **Look, read and listen. What is the text about? Circle the correct answer.**

a a sport b a person c a house

A skateboarder's dream

This house is a perfect house for skateboarders. There aren't any carpets, plants, pictures or posters on the walls in this house. Why? Think about it!

Normally people skateboard in the park or in the garden. In this house people skateboard inside! They skateboard in the living room, in the kitchen, in the bedroom and in the bathroom. They skateboard on the walls too!

Look at the living room. There's a table, some chairs, an armchair and a sofa with some cushions. It looks typical, but people skateboard on the sofa, tables and chairs!

There's a big skateboard practice room too. People train with friends and they have competitions there. It's really cool!

It's a skateboarder's dream house.

4 Read the sentences. Circle *yes*, *no* or *no info*.

1 People skateboard inside the house.
   (yes) / no / no info
2 There's a TV in the living room.
   yes / no / no info
3 There are cushions in the living room.
   yes / no / no info
4 There are three sofas in the living room.
   yes / no / no info
5 There's a carpet in the bedroom.
   yes / no / no info
6 There's a big skateboard practice room.
   yes / no / no info

5 Read the text again and answer the questions.

1 What rooms are there in the house?
2 What objects are there in the house?
3 What objects in Exercise 1 are **not** in the house?

6 Imagine your dream house. Write five sentences about it in your notebook. Tell your partner.

There are … rooms. There's a … and there are …
In my … there is a small/big …

3.6 Listening and Writing

I can understand and write short texts about bedrooms.

1 **Look at photos A–C. Find these objects in the photos. Which is your favourite bedroom? Why?**

chair cushion desk plant wardrobe

A

B

C

2 **Exam Spot** 2.12 **Listen and match the speakers to their bedrooms. Write A, B or C. There is one extra photo.**

☐ Speaker 1 ☐ Speaker 2

3 2.12 **Complete the sentences with a preposition of place. Then listen again and check.**

Speaker 1

1 My bed is *next to* the window.
2 My school things are ______ the desk.
3 There's an orange chair ______ my desk.
4 There are orange cushions ______ the bed.

Speaker 2

5 My clothes are ______ the wardrobe.
6 There are two beds ______ my bedroom.
7 The beds are ______ the wardrobe.
8 There aren't any posters ______ the walls.

4 **In pairs, describe one of the photos in Exercise 1 for a partner to guess.**

5 **The bedroom in Photo A is Lucas's. Read his blog post about it. What isn't there in the bedroom?**

My bedroom

'My bed is next to a green wall. There are two cushions and a toy on my bed. There's a big white desk. It's next to the window. There's a chair too. It's black and it's very cool. There's a computer and a lamp on the desk. My room is great!'

Writing Apostrophes

Remember to use apostrophes with contractions.

there is = there's is not = isn't are not = aren't
it is = it's they are = they're that is = that's

6 **Add apostrophes to these sentences.**

1 There isn't a desk in my bedroom.
2 Theres a plant.
3 Its under the bed.
4 There arent any books.

7 **Writing Time** **Write about your bedroom.**

Find ideas
Make a list of objects in your bedroom.
Write where they are.

Draft
Write about your bedroom.
Give your text a title.
My bed's …
There's / There isn't a …
There are / There aren't any …

Check and write
Check the apostrophes and write the final version of your text.

Vocabulary

1 Work in pairs. Student A: Choose a square. Student B: Say where you can find the object. Then swap roles.

A: *3B*

B: *'Wardrobe' … There's a big wardrobe in my bedroom!*

	1	2	3	4
A	bath	bed	desk	door
B	fridge	sofa	wardrobe	chair
C	lamp	window	table	cushion

2 Read the riddles. Write the objects.

1 There are three on my bedroom wall. p*osters*
2 It's on the floor in the living room. c______
3 It's in the living room. There's a film on it now! T______
4 They're green. They are in my garden. p______
5 I sit in it when I read a book. a______

3 Look at the picture. Read and complete the sentences with a preposition of place.

1 There are cushions *on* the beds.
2 There's a sofa ________ the living room.
3 There's a plant ________ the sofa.
4 There's a skateboard ________ the fridge.
5 The cat is ________ the door.
6 The trainers are ________ the bed.

Pronunciation

4 2.13 Listen and repeat: /ɪ/ or /iː/?

There are sixteen TVs in the living room
And three big fridges in the kitchen!

Grammar

5 Look at the picture in Exercise 3. Complete the text with *there is, there isn't, there are* or *there aren't*.

[1] *There are* five rooms in the house. [2] ________ a living room and there's a kitchen. [3] ________ a bathroom and [4] ________ two bedrooms. [5] ________ a garden but there's a garage. [6] ________ any windows in the garage.

6 Write questions about the house in Exercise 3. Use *Is there* or *Are there* and the words in brackets.

1 *Is there a table* (a table) in the living room?
2 ____________ (a TV) in the kitchen?
3 ____________ (plants) in the bedroom?
4 ____________ (a skateboard) in the kitchen?
5 ____________ (cushions) in the bathroom?

7 Answer the questions in Exercise 6.

1 *Yes, there is.*

Communication

8 Complete the dialogues with the words in the box.

please | Where's | show | ~~Hi~~ | upstairs | Would | come in

1 **Mariana:** [1] *Hi* Louise. Please, [2] ________!
Louise: Thanks.
Mariana: [3] ________ you like a drink?
Louise: Yes, [4] ________.

2 **Louise:** [5] ________ your room, Mariana?
Mariana: It's [6] ________. Let me [7] ________ you.

Check yourself!

- I can talk about my house. ☐
- I can use prepositions of place. ☐
- I can use *there is / there are*. ☐
- I can ask for something. ☐
- I can ask where something is. ☐

Get Culture!

Houses in the UK

1 **There are different types of houses in the UK. In pairs, talk about where you can find these types of houses.**

a in the city **b** in the country
c in the city and in the country

2 🔊 **2.14** **Read the texts and circle the type of the house Ian, Lisa and Claire live in. Then listen and check.**

Tell me where you live

Ian, 10

I live in a *houseboat* / *semi-detached house*. The boys next door and I are friends. There's a big tree in their garden. In the tree there's a tree-house. We play there all the time!

Lisa, 12

I live in a *block of flats* / *detached house* with twelve floors. Our flat isn't very big. There are two small bedrooms but the living room is nice. The view is fantastic!

Claire, 11

We live in the city, in a street with *terraced houses* / *cottages*. They are all tall and grey but the doors are different colours. Our door is yellow!

3 🔊 **2.15** **Listen and complete the texts with the words in the box.**

behind	cottage	~~country~~	view
houseboat	small		

Martha, 12

My family and I live in the [1] *country*. Our house is a [2] ________ in Devon, South England. There are lots of trees [3] ________ our house.

Matt, 13

I live in a [4] ________ on the River Thames. It is very [5] ________ but I like it. The [6] ________ is always different!

4 **Write a short text about where you live. Use texts in Exercises 2 and 3 to help you.**

I live in a block of flats. Our living room is big and the view from it is amazing.

Hampton Court Palace

A ▶18 **Watch the video and answer the presenter's questions. Then circle the correct answer.**

Hampton Court was the home of ____ VIII.

a King Charles b Queen Elizabeth c King Henry

B ▶18 **Watch the video again. Complete the sentences with one word from the video.**

1 Hampton Court Palace is in ______ .
2 There are ______ kings or queens in Hampton Court today.
3 There are over 1,000 ______ in Hampton Court.
4 The Great Hall is a big room for ______ and parties.
5 The maze in the ______ of Hampton Court is very old.

C Discuss in pairs. Which part of Hampton Court Palace is your favourite? Why?

PROJECT

- **Work in groups. Make a digital presentation of an unusual or interesting house in your area.**
- **Take photos of the house or find them on the Internet.**
- **Write a description of the house. Use these questions to help you.**

  Where is the house?
  What type of house is it?
  Is it big/small?
  What colour is it?
  Is there a garden/garage?

- **Put the photos and text together.**
- **Share your presentation with the class. Which is your favourite house? Why?**

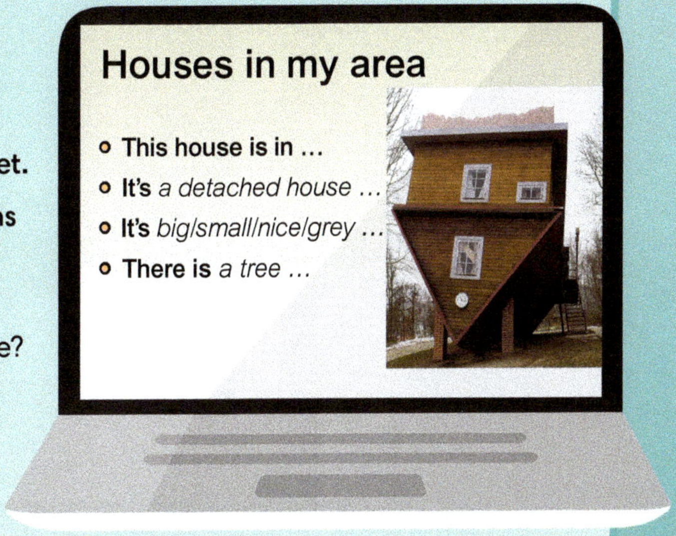

4 About me

Vocabulary I can describe someone's face and hair.

In this unit

Vocabulary
- Face and hair
- Parts of the body
- Personality adjectives

Grammar
- *have got* affirmative and negative
- Regular and irregular plural
- *have got* questions and short answers
- Possessive adjectives

19–20 4.2 Grammar video

21 4.2 Grammar animation

22 4.3 Grammar animation

23 4.4 Communication video

I know that!

1 Say the words and point at the features of your face.

ears eyes hair mouth nose

2 2.16 **Listen and repeat. Find the features in the photos on page 46.**

Vocabulary Face and hair

Face

ears eyes mouth nose teeth

Hair

curly spiky straight wavy
blond dark red

3 **Find the numbers (1–6) in the photos on page 46. Write whose features they are.**

1 They're *Sammy's ears* .
2 They're __________ .
3 It's __________ .
4 It's __________ .
5 They're __________ .
6 It's __________ .

4 **In pairs, write the words in the box in the correct place. You can use them more than once.**

big blond blue brown curly dark green grey long red short small spiky straight wavy white

1 eyes	*blue*
2 ears / nose / mouth	
3 hair	
4 teeth	

LOOK! Maria's hair **is** brown.

5 **Look at the photos on page 46. Circle the correct answer.**

1 Regan's eyes are *(brown)* / *green*.
2 Sammy's hair is *straight* / *curly*.
3 Maria's hair is *long* / *short*.
4 Antek's hair is *spiky* / *wavy*.
5 Sammy's hair is *blond* / *dark*.
6 Regan's hair is *short* / *wavy*.
7 Antek's eyes are *blue* / *brown*.

6 **Look at the children's hair. Complete the words.**

a [ ]

straight

b [ ]

w _ _ y

c [ ]

_ u _ l _

d [ ]

_ _ ik _

e [*1*]

l _ _ g

f [ ]

_ h _ r _

7 2.17 **Listen and number the pictures in Exercise 6.**

LOOK!
long/short curly/straight blond/brown/red hair
big/small blue/brown eyes

8 **Which words in Exercise 4 describe your hair and eyes? Write them down. Use Look! box to help you. Tell a partner.**

__________ __________ __________ hair
__________ __________ eyes

9 **In pairs, describe someone in your class. Guess who it is.**

A: *Long straight brown hair, brown eyes.*
B: *It's Alice!*

I remember that!

10 **Do you know a person with …**

a green eyes? *my mum*
b spiky hair? __________
c grey hair? __________
d a small nose? __________

4.2 Grammar

I can use the affirmative and negative forms of the verb *have got*.

I haven't got big feet!

At the bookshop.

Alex: Ouch, my foot! Be careful!
Jen: It isn't my fault! You've got long legs! And you've got big feet!
Alex: I haven't got big feet! I'm tall!

Jen: You've got long arms too! Like this!
Alex: Yeah, but I haven't got a big head, like you!

Jen: My head is fine! Mum? Is my head big?
Mum: Stop it, you two! Jen, your brother hasn't got big feet. Alex, your sister hasn't got a big head! Now, hurry up with the books! We haven't got a lot of time.

Jen: Oh, they've got *Yummy Cupcakes* Great! Oh, no! It's too high! Alex? Help me, please!

1 ▶19 🔊 2.18 **Watch or listen and read. Jen needs Alex's help. Why? Finish the sentence.**

Because the book is too ______ .

2 Circle the correct answer.

1 (*Jen*) / *Alex* isn't careful.
2 *Alex* / *Jen* is tall.
3 Alex's arms are *long* / *short*.
4 Jen's head isn't *big* / *fine*.
5 Jen's book is about *cupcakes* / *big feet*.

3 🔊 2.19 **Listen and read. Find these expressions in the story.**

Say it

It isn't my fault! Stop it!
Help me, please!

4 ▶ Guess! **Will Alex help Jen? Have a class vote.**

5 ▶20 🔊 2.20 **Now watch or listen and check.**

Grammar *have got* affirmative and negative

▶ 21 **Get Grammar!**

+ Short and long form	– Short and long form
I've (have) got long legs.	I haven't (have not) got long legs.
You've (have) got long legs.	You haven't (have not) got long legs.
He/She/It's (has) got long legs.	He/She/It hasn't (has not) got long legs.
We've (have) got long legs.	We haven't got (have not) got long legs.
You've (have) got long legs.	You haven't got (have not) got long legs.
They've (have) got long legs.	They haven't (have not) got long legs.

6 Complete the sentences with *'ve got* or *'s got*.

1 **Jen:** 'Alex, you *'ve got* big feet!'
2 **Jen:** 'Alex ______ long arms.'
3 **Alex:** 'Jen ______ a big head.'
4 **Mum:** 'We ______ very little time.'
5 **Jen:** 'They ______ *Yummy Cupcakes*.'

7 🔊 2.21 Listen and repeat.

Vocabulary Parts of the body

arm body fingers foot hand head
leg neck toes

8 Label the parts of the body.

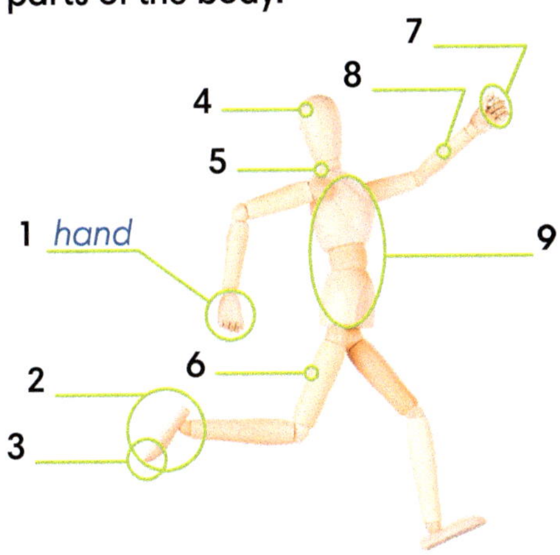

9 Write the correct sentences in your notebook.

1 Jen's got blond hair. (brown)
Jen hasn't got blond hair. She's got brown hair.
2 Alex's got small feet. (big)
3 Jen and Alex have got short legs. (long)
4 Their mum's got blue eyes. (brown)
5 Jen and Alex have got big heads. (small)

LOOK!
finger – fingers foot – feet
toe – toes tooth – teeth

10 **Exam Spot** Look at Ike and Mike. Complete the text with one word in each gap.

big got they has tall feet ~~have~~

Ike and Mike [1]*have* got long spiky hair. [2]______ 've got big mouths but they haven't got [3]______ noses. Mike is [4]______ . He [5]______ got green hair. He's [6]______ very long arms and very big [7]______ .

11 Write about Ike. Use Exercise 10 to help you.
Ike isn't tall. He's got …

Fun Spot

12 Create a friend for Ike and Mike. Give her a name and describe her.
Ike and Mike have got a friend.
She's got … and …
She's got … but she hasn't got …

4.3 Grammar

I can ask questions with the verb *have got* and use *its, our, your* and *their*.

The Terrific Two My favourite superhero

1 Look at the cartoon. Someone looks like Superdug. Where is this person?

2 2.22 Listen and read. Who is Wonder Will?

3 Read the sentences. Circle T (true) or F (false).

1 Superdug is at home. T / F
2 Superdug hasn't got a super car. T / F
3 X1 and X2 have got super ears. T / F
4 Kit's got super eyes. T / F
5 X1 and X2 haven't got any battery power now. T / F

Grammar *have got* questions and short answers

▶ 22 **Get Grammar!**

?	Short answers
Have I got a friend?	Yes, I have. / No, I haven't.
Have you got a friend?	Yes, you have. / No, you haven't.
Has he/she/it got a friend?	Yes, he/she/it has. / No, he/she/it hasn't.
Have we got a friend?	Yes, we have. / No, we haven't.
Have you got a friend?	Yes, you have. / No, you haven't.
Have they got a friend?	Yes, they have. / No, they haven't.

What have you got? I've got super powers!

4 **Complete the questions with *have … got* or *has … got*.**

1 *Has* Wonder Will *got* a red suit?
2 ____ Ricky ____ blue hair?
3 ____ X1 and X2 ____ big heads?
4 ____ Kit ____ brown eyes?
5 ____ X1 and X2 ____ long legs?
6 ____ Superdug ____ long ears?

5 **Look at the cartoon. Answer the questions in Exercise 4.**

1 *No, he hasn't.*

6 **In pairs, ask and answer about the superheroes.**

	super eyes	super ears	super arms
 Wondercat	✔	✔	✘
 Iron Girls	✔	✘	✔

A: *Has Wondercat got super eyes?*
B: *Yes, she has.*

LOOK!

it → its		The robot hasn't got its battery.
we → our		Superdug is our favourite hero!
you → your		They are your robots.
they → their		Wonder Will is their friend.

7 **Complete the sentences with *our, your* or *their*.**

1 They've got green super suits.
These are *their* super suits.
2 We've got a super car!
This is ____ super car!
3 You've got a new robot!
This is ____ new robot.
4 Have they got a super cat?
Is this ____ super cat?
5 Has it got a super battery?
Is this ____ super battery?

8 **Work in pairs. Ask your partner what he/she has got. Answer your partner's questions. Use the words in the box. Then tell the class about your partner.**

a brother or a sister? a pet? a TV in your room?
a ruler? a friend? a hobby? a bike? a robot?

A: *Have you got a brother or a sister?*

9 2.23 2.24
Go to page 107.
Listen and sing Robots' Song.

Fun Spot

4.4 Communication

I can say sorry and respond to an apology.

Sorry about that!

Dad: Where are my house keys?
Jen: I'm so sorry, Dad. I've got them.
Dad: It's OK. Now, where's my phone? Oops! Sorry, Jen!
Jen: That's all right.
Dad: Are you OK?
Jen: Yes, I'm fine.

Jen: Dad! You've got the phone! It's right there!
Dad: Sorry, my mistake!
Jen: No problem.
Dad: Oh, it's late! Bye, Jen!

Jen: Dad, wait! Your house keys!
Dad: Oh, dear! Sorry about that! Thanks, sweetie! Bye!
Jen: Bye, Dad!

Jen: Come on, really? Erm … Dad?

1 23 2.25 Watch or listen and read. Who has got Dad's phone? Circle the correct answer.

a Jen b Dad

2 2.26 Listen and repeat.

Communication Apologising

A:	B:
I'm so sorry.	It's OK.
Sorry about that!	That's all right.
Sorry, my mistake.	No problem.
Are you OK?	I'm fine.

3 2.27 Complete the dialogues. Then listen and check. Act out the dialogues in pairs.

1 A: Oops! Sorry about that, Pete! B: No *problem*.
A: Are you sure? B: Yes, I'm ______ .

2 A: Where's my phone? B: ______ , I've got it!
A: That's ______ .

3 A: This isn't my jacket. B: Sorry, my ______ .
A: ______ OK. Thanks. Here you are.

4 **Exam Spot** Draw lines from the sentences to the pictures. There is one extra sentence.

1 *That's all right.*

2 *Oh, sorry about that!*

3 *This isn't my bag.*

5 Game! Make dialogues in pairs. Don't stop. The pair that talks the longest wins the game.

A: *Where's my bag?*
B: *I'm so sorry. I've got it. Where are my keys?*

I can understand and do a personality quiz. Reading 4.5

1 🔊 2.28 **Listen and repeat. Complete the sentences with the words in the Vocabulary box.**

Vocabulary Personality adjectives

clever friendly funny helpful nice sporty

1 I speak to everyone. I'm *friendly* .
2 My teacher helps me every day. She's _______ .
3 You've got flowers for your mum. You're very _______ .
4 My friend's jokes are great! He's _______ .
5 They love football and tennis. They're _______ .
6 I've got good marks at school. I'm _______ .

2 **Do the personality quiz! Circle a, b or c.**

3 **Count how many a, b and c answers you have got and read the key. Do you agree? Tell a friend or the class!**

4 🔊 2.29 **Listen to two friends. Are they friendly, funny and sporty? Tick (✔) for *yes* and put a cross (✗) for *no*.**

	friendly	funny	sporty
Sam	✔		
Sue			

Fun Spot

5 **Write about a student from your class. Read the text out. Can the class guess who it is?**

A: *This student is very friendly and she's sporty. She's very helpful too.*
B: *Is it Maria?*
A: *Yes! You're right!*

QUIZ TIME Do our personality quiz to find out!

1 How many good friends have you got?
 a 3–6 **b** 7–10 **c** 1 or 2

2 Are your jokes funny?
 a Sometimes. **b** Yes! **c** No. My jokes are bad!

3 What's your favourite hobby?
 a Sports. **b** Dancing. **c** Reading.

4 What's your favourite place?
 a School. **b** A party! **c** My room.

5 Are you good at school?
 a I'm OK. **b** Yes, I am!
 c I'm good at my favourite subjects.

6 Your best friend has got a problem. You:
 a help your friend. **b** just say 'I'm sorry'.
 c say 'Speak to your mum'.

7 Your neighbour has got a big bag. You say:
 a 'Hello, I can help!' **b** 'That's big!'
 c 'I'm sorry, I've got homework.'

Key:

A lot of your answers are **a**.

GOOD FRIEND!
You are a good friend. You are very nice! You are helpful and sporty. You are a good student.

A lot of your answers are **b**.

PARTY ANIMAL!
You are very funny and friendly but you aren't always very helpful. Jokes, parties and dancing are your favourite things but you are also a good student.

A lot of your answers are **c**.

HOME LOVER!
You are friendly … sometimes! You don't like groups. You aren't very sporty but you are usually a good student.

4.6 Listening and Writing

I can understand and write short texts about cartoon characters

1

2

3

4

1 Look at the photos. Can you name the cartoons?

2 2.30 Find the characters in the photos. Write the correct number. There is one extra photo. Then listen and check.

☐ Skipper ☐ Kevin
☐ SpongeBob SquarePants

3 2.31 Listen to the dialogue and tick (✔) the children's opinion.

	SpongeBob SquarePants	Kevin	Skipper
funny	✔		
helpful			
friendly			
clever			

4 2.31 Complete the sentences with the words in the box. Then listen and check.

isn't ~~clever~~ Kevin cool ideas

1 SpongeBob SquarePants isn't very *clever*.
2 All Minions are ________ .
3 ________ loves bananas and apples.
4 Skipper has got good ________ .
5 Sometimes Skipper ________ nice or friendly.

5 Who is your favourite cartoon character? Describe him/her to a friend.

6 Read Lian's web text about her favourite cartoon character. Do you know it?

Paragraph 1
Kung Fu Panda's name is Po. He's got a big body and head. He's got big blue eyes and small black ears. They're cool. His legs are short and his arms are long. He's got brown shorts.

Paragraph 2
I think Po is nice. He's funny and he's friendly. He's got lots of friends. He's clever and he's sporty too. He's very good at kung fu!

Writing Paragraphs

A paragraph is a part of a text. It's about one main idea. Remember to divide your text into paragraphs!

7 Read Lian's web text again. Write the paragraph numbers. Add examples from Lian's text to each paragraph.

☐ Face and body *big body, big head, …*
☐ Personality *nice, …*

8 Writing Time Write about your favourite character from a book or cartoon.

Find ideas

Find a photo of your character.
Make a list of words describing his/her face, body and personality.

Draft

1 Write a paragraph about his/her face and body.
(Your character's name) has got a really friendly face. …
2 Write a paragraph about his/her personality.
He/She isn't very clever but …

Check and write

Check the paragraphs and write the final version of your text.

Vocabulary

1 **Look at Maddy. Write words 1–9 describing her body. Then complete words a–e describing her face.**

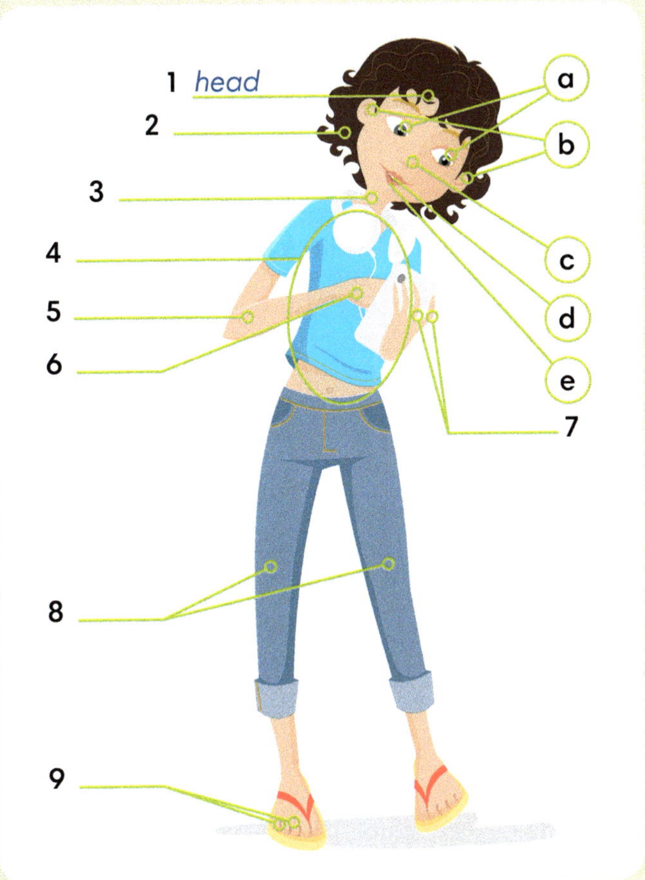

a e*y*e*e*s b e_ _s c n_ _e
d t_ _ _h e m_u_ _

2 **Read sentences 1–3 about Maddy's hair. Tick (✔) the sentence that is true.**

1 ☐ She's got long dark straight hair.
2 ☐ She's got short blond curly hair.
3 ☐ She's got short brown wavy hair.

3 **Match the word fragments to make five adjectives.**

fun 1 (— ny)
cle 2
help 3
spor 4
friend 5
ni 6

ce
ty
ly
ny
ver
ful

Pronunciation

4 🔊 2.32 **Listen and repeat: /h/.**

Her name's Helpful Helen, her horse's name is Claire.
Her home is in Hastings. She's got white hair!

Grammar

5 **Write questions in your notebook.**

1 Have eyes you brown got ?
Have you got brown eyes?
2 curly your hair dad Has got ?
3 you and your friends dark hair Have got ?
4 your mum eyes Has got blue ?
5 Have a car your parents got ?
6 a pet got your grandparents Have ?

6 **Answer the questions in Exercise 5.**

1 *Yes, I have. / No, I haven't.*

7 **Complete the sentences with *its, our, your* or *their*.**

1 *Our* (we) names are Jo and Alex.
2 This is ______ (they) new house.
3 Where is ______ (you) homework?
4 Is it your dog? What's ______ name?

Communication

8 **Complete the dialogues with the words in the box.**

problem	That's	~~mistake~~	so	Sorry	It's OK

1 A: Where's my phone?
B: I've got it. Sorry, my [1] *mistake* .
A: [2] ______ all right.

2 B: Ooops! I've got your cap. [3] ______ about that.
A: No [4] ______ .

3 A: I haven't got your book today. I'm [5] ______ sorry.
B: [6] ______ .

Check yourself! ✔

- I can describe someone's face and hair. ☐
- I can use the verb *have got*. ☐
- I can use possessive adjectives *its, our, your* and *their*. ☐
- I can say sorry and respond to an apology. ☐

Reading and Writing

What's your favourite place? Write about it!

Bev, 11

1 My favourite place is my granny's house. It's a small cottage in the country. My favourite room is the living room. There are a lot of old things there. There are old books, lamps and some of my old toys!

Jane, 10

2 My favourite place is my classroom! It's very big. There are long, white desks. We've all got our own box for our books and schoolbags. We can play computer games with the teacher on the white board too. It's so cool.

Julieta, 13

3 My favourite place is our home in the country. I go there with my mum, dad and sister at weekends. There are two small bedrooms and a living room. There is a bathroom behind our home. There's a kitchen in the house too but we cook outside. It's fun!

1 **Work in pairs. Say what you can see in the photos.**

2 **Read and match texts 1–3 to photos A–C.**

3 **Read the sentences. Circle *yes*, *no* or *no info*.**

1 Bev's house is in the country. yes / no / no info

2 There are toys in the living room. yes / no / no info

3 Jane's classroom is small. yes / no / no info

4 All the students in Jane's class have got a computer. yes / no / no info

5 Julieta's home in the country has got four rooms. yes / no / no info

6 The kitchen is outside. yes / no / no info

4 Exam Spot **Write about 40–50 words about your favourite place. Use these questions to help you.**

1 What is your favourite place?

2 Where is this place?

3 What is inside / next to it?

4 Who is there?

5 What is nice about it?

My favourite place is … It's in … There are … in my favourite place. There is a nice … / There are nice …

5 Exam Spot **Look and read. Write *yes* or *no*.**

1 The boy has got short, spiky hair. *yes*

2 There is a brown carpet on the floor. ______

3 The man has got long arms. ______

4 There aren't any jumpers. ______

5 There are six hoodies. ______

6 The girl is sporty. ______

Listening

6 **Exam Spot** 2.33 **Listen and draw lines. There is one extra picture.**

Communication

7 **Exam Spot** **Read the sententces and circle the best answer.**

1 **Jane:** Hi, come in!
Peter: a No problem. b Are you OK? (c) Thanks.

2 **Jane:** Would you like a cupcake?
Peter: a She's in the kitchen.
b It's too small.
c No, thanks.

3 **Peter:** Where's your brother?
Jane: a He's upstairs.
b He's got a new computer.
c They're at school.

4 **Peter:** Oh no! My juice is on the sofa … .
Jane: a I'm fine, thanks.
b That's all right.
c It's nice.

5 **Peter:** Where's the bathroom, please?
Jane: a It's next to the kitchen. Let me show you.
b This is the living room.
c All right.

8 **Exam Spot** **Work in pairs. Ask and answer the questions.**

1 Who is your favourite person in your family?
2 Where do you do your homework?
3 What's in your living room?

Exam Language Bank

Parts of the house
bathroom, bedroom, door, floor, garage, garden, kitchen, living room, wall, window

Face
ears, eyes, mouth, nose, teeth

Inside the house
armchair, bath, bed, chair, desk, fridge, sofa, table, wardrobe

Hair
curly, spiky, straight, wavy, blond, dark, red

Prepositions of place
behind, in, in front of, next to, on, under

Household objects
carpet, cushion, lamp, plant, poster, television (TV)

Parts of the body
arm, body, fingers, foot, hand, head, leg, neck, toes

Personality adjectives
clever, friendly, funny, helpful, nice, sporty

Having a guest
Hello. Please, come in.
Thank you.
Would you like *a sandwich*?
Yes, please. / No, thanks.
Where's the *bathroom*, please?
It's *upstairs/downstairs*.
It's next to the *living room*.
Let me show you.

Apologising
I'm so sorry.
Sorry about that!
Sorry, my mistake.
Are you OK?

It's OK.
That's all right.
No problem.
I'm fine.

5 Things I can do

Vocabulary I can understand action verbs.

In this unit

Vocabulary
- Action verbs
- Collocations with *make*, *play* and *ride*

Grammar
- *can* affirmative, negative, questions and short answers

24–25

5.2 Grammar video

26

5.2 Grammar animation

27

5.3 Grammar animation

28

5.4 Communication video

29

BBC Culture video

I know that!

1 Find these actions in the photos.

climb draw jump ride a bike run skateboard swim

1

2

3

4

5

6

7

2 2.34 Listen and repeat. Which actions are not in the photos on page 58?

Vocabulary Action verbs

act climb cook dive draw fix
fly jump read ride run sing
skateboard swim write

3 Label the illustrations with words in the Vocabulary box.

1 cook

2 ______

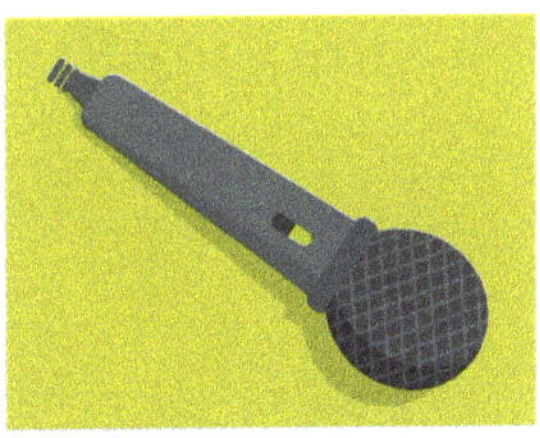

3 ______

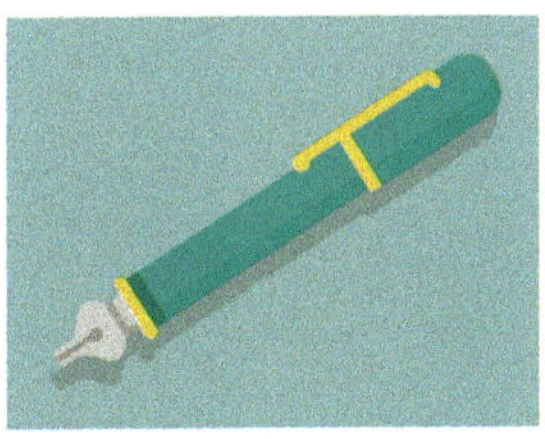

4 ______

5 ______

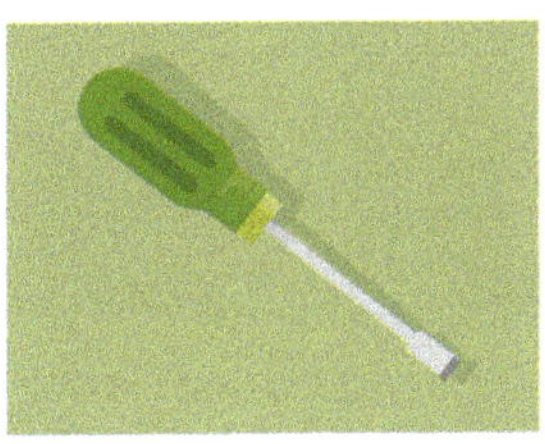

6 ______

7 ______

8 ______

4 2.35 Listen and circle the action you hear.

1 write / (read)
2 swim / cook
3 draw / ride
4 write / skateboard
5 run / dive
6 act / sing

5 Exam Spot Which actions are in the picture? Tick (✔) for *yes* or put a cross (✗) for *no*.

1 [✔] swim
2 [ ] dive
3 [ ] read
4 [ ] jump
5 [ ] draw
6 [ ] fix
7 [ ] ride
8 [ ] fly

6 Work in pairs. Look at the picture in Exercise 5. Mime actions for your partner to guess!

7 In pairs, complete the groups of words.

1 Things we do at school: read, write, draw
2 Things actors do: ______
3 Sports: ______
4 Hobbies: ______
5 Things we do at home: ______
6 Things we do in the water: ______
7 Things birds do: ______

I remember that!

8 Make two lists that are true for you. Use the Vocabulary box to help you.

I think it's easy to: cook, ______.
I think it's difficult to: ______.

5.2 Grammar

I can use the verb *can* in affirmative and negative sentences.

I can fix it!

Lian: Guys, this video is for my granny, in Shanghai. Granny Lin, this is my friend, Lucas.
Lucas: Hello!
Lian: Lucas is very talented! He can play the guitar and he can sing!
Lucas: Well, I can't sing very well but …

Lian: Oh no, not again!
Alex: What's wrong?
Lian: It's the camera. I can't see a thing!
Alex: Let me see … Hmm, I can fix it.
Lian: Thanks! Alex is a genius! He can fix things! He can do very clever things with computers too!

Jen: Yes, very clever – he can play computer games all day! Cupcake?
Lian: Jen is a fantastic cook! These cupcakes are yummy!

Alex: But what about Lian?
Lucas: Yes, what can she do?

1 ▶ 24 🔊 2.36 **Watch or listen and read. Finish the sentence.**

There's something wrong with Lian's ________ .

2 Complete the sentences.

1 The video is for *Lian's granny* .
2 Lian's granny is in ________ .
3 ________ is very talented.
4 ________ is a genius.
5 ________ is a good cook.

3 🔊 2.37 **Listen and repeat. Find these expressions in the story.**

Say it!

Not again!   What's wrong?   Let me see …

4 **Guess!** **Look at the story again. What can Lian do?**

Lian can ________ , ________ and ________ .

5 ▶ 25 🔊 2.38 **Now watch or listen and check.**

Grammar *can* affirmative and negative

▶ 26 **Get Grammar!**

+	–
I **can** jump.	I **can't** jump.
You **can** jump.	You **can't** jump.
He/She/It **can** jump.	He/She/It **can't** jump.
We **can** jump.	We **can't** jump.
You **can** jump.	You **can't** jump.
They **can** jump.	They **can't** jump.

6 **Write who can do these things. Then look at the photos on page 60 and check.**

Lian (x2) Jen (x2) Alex (x1) Lucas (x2)

1 *Lian* *can* skateboard.
2 ______ ______ sing.
3 ______ ______ make cupcakes.
4 ______ ______ draw.
5 ______ ______ cook.
6 ______ ______ fix things.
7 ______ ______ play the guitar.

7 **Follow the lines and write what they can't do. Read the sentences.**

1 Lian *can't* *fix things* .
2 Jen *can't* ______ .
3 Alex ______ ______ .
4 Lucas ______ ______ .
5 Lian ______ ______ .
6 Alex ______ ______ .

draw
cook
play the guitar
fix things
skateboard
sing

8 2.39 **Listen and circle *can* or *can't*.**

1 He *can* / *can't* swim.
2 She *can* / *can't* draw.
3 They *can* / *can't* act.
4 He *can* / *can't* sing.
5 She *can* / *can't* run.
6 His brother *can* / *can't* read.

9 2.40 **Listen and repeat.**

Vocabulary *make, play, ride*

make a poster / cupcakes
play computer games / football / the piano
ride a bike / a horse

LOOK! play football
play **the** piano

10 **Complete Lucas's email with *can* and *make*, *play* or *ride*.**

To: Ben

My family is very talented! My dad [1]*can play* football very well. My mum [2]__________ a horse and she [3]__________ the piano. My aunt Melina [4]__________ cupcakes. They're yummy! As for me, I [5]__________ the guitar and I [6]__________ a bike!

11 **Work in pairs.**
Student A: Write three true and three false sentences.
Student B: Guess which sentences are true.
Then swap roles.

A: *I can play the guitar.*
B: *It's true. / It's false.*

Fun Spot

5.3 Grammar I can ask and answer questions with the verb *can*.

The Terrific Two Thank you, Superdug

1 Look at the cartoon and answer the questions.

1 What's the title of Dug's book?
2 Who can swim in the cartoon?

2 2.41 Listen and read. Finish the sentence.

The woman is Tom and Susan's ________ .

3 Read the cartoon again and complete the sentences with one word.

1 Dug can *see* the boat over there.
2 Susan and Tom are in the ________ .
3 Susan and Tom can't ________ .
4 Kit and Superdug ________ help.
5 Superdug can't swim but he can ________ .

Grammar *can* questions and short answers

▶ 27 **Get Grammar!**

?	Short answers
Can I swim?	Yes, I can. / No I can't.
Can you swim?	Yes, you can. / No, you can't.
Can he/she/it swim?	Yes, he/she/it can. / No, he/she/it can't.
Can we swim?	Yes, we can. / No, we can't.
Can you swim?	Yes, you can. / No, you can't.
Can they swim?	Yes, they can. / No, they can't.
What can we do?	We can help.

4 In your notebook, write questions and short answers.

1 fly Can Superdug ?

Can Superdug fly? Yes, he can.

2 Dug fly Can ?

3 Tom and Susan Can fly ?

4 the boat you see Can ?

5 Can swim the little dog ?

5 Look at the cartoon. Ask and answer the questions in pairs.

1 **Picture 2** Dug / see the children?

A: *Can Dug see the children?*

B: *Yes, he can.*

2 **Picture 3** Tom and Susan / swim?

3 **Picture 3** What / Kit and Dug / do?

4 **Picture 4** Superdug / run fast?

5 **Picture 4** Superdug / swim?

6 In pairs, ask and answer about Kit and Dug.

swim?	✔	✘
draw?	✘	✔
cook?	✔	✘

A: *Can Kit swim?* B: *Yes, she can.*

7 Copy the table. Add your idea for number 5. Ask five of your classmates. How many of them *can* or *can't* do these things?

Can you …	1	2	3	4	5
1 swim?	✔	✔	✘	✘	✘
2 fix a computer?					
3 ride a horse?					
4 draw?					
5 … ?					

8 Write a report of your survey in Exercise 7.

Two people can swim and three people can't swim!

Fun Spot

9 2.42 2.43

Go to page 107.
Listen and chant the Activities Rap.

Let's do something fun!

Lucas: Hey, guys, let's do something fun.
Jen: I agree. Any ideas?
Alex: We can go to the park.
Jen: Again? It's not a good idea.
Lian: Let's go ice-skating.
Jen: Great idea!
Lucas: I'm not sure … I can't skate very well.
Lian: No problem. I can teach you.
Lucas: OK, cool! Let's do that!

Alex: Hey, Lucas? You can wear these!
Lucas: Ha, ha! You're so funny!

1 28 2.44 **Watch or listen and read. What do they decide to do? Tick (✔) the correct picture.**

1 ☐ 

2 ☐ 

3 ☐ 

2 2.45 **Listen and repeat.**

Communication Suggestions

A: Let's *do something fun*! / Let's *go ice-skating*!
We can *go to the park*!

B: 🙂 I agree! / Let's do that! / Great idea!
😐 I'm not sure.
☹ It's not a good idea.

3 Complete the sentences with one word.

1 We *can* go to the cinema!
2 _____ go to the beach!
3 Let's _____ something fun!
4 _____ can play football!
5 We _____ ride our bikes!

4 Exam Spot **Circle the best answer.**

1 A: Let's do something fun.
B: a Let me see … b I agree. Any ideas? c What's wrong?

2 A: Let's go to the swimming pool!
B: a We can go to the park. b Let's do something fun. c I'm not sure … I can't swim very well.

3 A: I can teach you.
B: a No problem. b OK. Let's do that! c You're so funny.

5 Read and answer. Use expressions in the Communication box.

1 A: We can make cupcakes! B: 🙂 *Great idea!*
2 A: Let's do something fun! B: 🙂
3 A: We can go to the park. B: ☹
4 A: Let's go to the zoo. B: 😐

6 In pairs, make dialogues like those in Exercise 5. Use the ideas in the box and add your own.

go to the cinema go to the swimming pool make a video play computer games play volleyball ride our bikes

A: *Let's ride our bikes!*
B: *I agree!*

I can understand a text about sign language. **Reading** 5.5

1 **Look at the photos and the title of the text. Do you know anyone who speaks sign language?**

2 2.46 **Read and listen to the text. Match headings a–d to paragraphs 1–4.**

a Learn sign language!
b A special language
c Where is sign language important?
d What is sign language?

3 **Read the sentences. Circle T (true) or F (false).**

1 People who can't hear have got a special language. (T)/ F
2 There is one sign language. T / F
3 There is one sign language alphabet. T / F
4 Sign language isn't important at home. T / F
5 Some TV programmes are in sign language. T / F

4 **The pictures show a certain word in British Sign Language alphabet. Go to page 106 and check the word. Can you show it with your hands?**

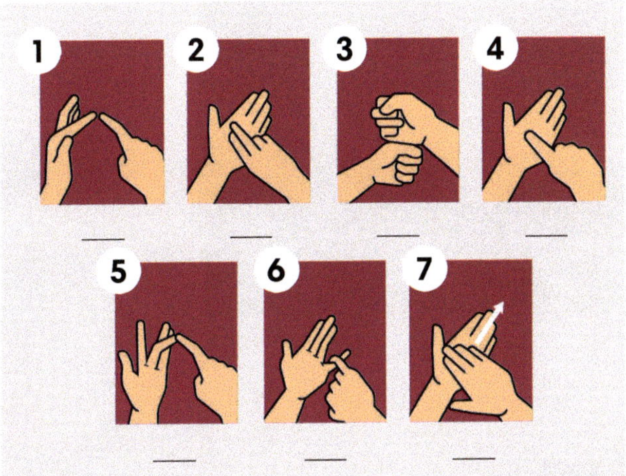

Sign language

1 b At school you can learn different languages, like English, French or Spanish. But there are special schools where teachers and students speak a sign language.

2 ☐ In sign language you can make letters and words with your hands. It's for people who can't hear. There are different sign languages and different sign language alphabets.

3 ☐ Sign language is important in schools and at home. All the family can learn sign language. They can speak to children who can't hear. Some TV programmes are in sign language too.

4 ☐ Are there children at your school who can't hear? You can learn sign language and make friends with them. There are sign language courses!

5.6 Listening and Writing

I can understand and write short texts about after-school clubs.

1 **Match photos 1–4 to after-school clubs a–d. In pairs, say what you can do in these clubs.**

1

2

3

4

a [4] swimming club
b [ ] art club
c [ ] drama club
d [ ] football club

2 2.47 **Listen to four children. Match speakers 1–4 to clubs a–d in Exercise 1.**

Speaker 1 [b]
Speaker 2 [ ]
Speaker 3 [ ]
Speaker 4 [ ]

3 Exam Spot 2.47 **Listen again. Complete with a number or an action verb.**

1 At art club you can learn to paint and *draw* .
2 The number of students in the art club is ______ .
3 In drama club they can teach you how to ______ .
4 Football club is for boys and girls from ten to ______ .
5 At swimming club kids can swim and ______ .

4 **Which of the clubs in Exercise 2 do you prefer? Have a class vote!**

5 **Read the ad for an after-school club. Who is the club for? Circle the correct answer.**

It's for students who like *sports / computers*.

Come to Computer Club!

You can make robots and you can play computer games too. How cool is that? You can write emails but you can't write computer programs? We can teach you.

Where: St Alban's Primary School
When: Monday, 4 o'clock

See you there!

www.U-and-Bot.get

Writing *and, but*

*You **can** make robots **and** you **can** play computer games.*
*You **can** write emails **but** you **can't** write computer programs.*

6 **Complete the sentences with *and* or *but*.**

1 I can run *and* I can jump.
2 She can sing ______ she can't act.
3 They can play computer games ______ make a robot ______ they can't write computer programs.

7 Writing Time **Write an ad for an after-school club.**

Find ideas

Make notes about what you can do at the club, and where and when the club is.

Draft

1 Write the title. *Come to … Club!*
2 Write a paragraph about what you can do at the club.
You can … and …
You can … but you can't …
3 Write where and when the club is.
Where: … When: … , … o'clock
4 Write the end. *See you there!*

Check and write

Check all the linkers (*and, but*) and write the final version of your text.

Vocabulary

1 Look at the picture and complete the action verbs 1–9. Then write six more action verbs in your notebook.

1 act	4 f_y	7 r_n
2 c_ _m_	5 j_ _p	8 s_ _g
3 f_x	6 r_ _d	9 s_ _m

2 Complete the collocations with *make*, *play* or *ride*.

1 make	cupcakes	4 ______	football
2 ______	a bike	5 ______	a horse
3 ______	the guitar	6 ______	a poster

Pronunciation

3 2.48 Listen and repeat: /ɑː/ or /æ/?

Mark's Aunt Ann can play the guitar
But she can't sing or act so she isn't a star!

Grammar

4 In your notebook, write sentences with *can* (✔) or *can't* (✘) and *and* or *but*.

1 Superdug / fly ✔ / swim ✘
Superdug can fly but he can't swim.
2 Leo / play the piano ✘ / play football ✔
3 I / make a cake ✘ / make a pizza ✔
4 You / play the guitar ✘ / sing ✘
5 They / skateboard ✔ / run very fast ✔

5 Complete the questions and short answers.

1 *Can you swim* (you / swim)? No, *I can't*.
2 ______ (David / sing) this song?
Yes, ______. He's very good.
3 ______ (the boys / act)?
No, ______!
4 Mum, ______ (we / play) a computer game?
No, ______. It's time for lunch.
5 ______ (you / see) Mario?
Yes, ______. He's over there.

Communication

6 Put the dialogue in the correct order. Then act it out in pairs.

a ☐ **B:** I'm not sure … I can't play very well.
b ☐ **B:** OK, cool. Let's do that.
c ☐ **B:** I agree. Any ideas?
d 1 **A:** Let's do something fun.
e ☐ **A:** No problem. I can teach you.
f ☐ **A:** We can play football.

Check yourself! ☑

- I can understand action verbs. ☐
- I can use collocations with *make*, *play* and *ride*. ☐
- I can use the verb *can* in affirmative and negative sentences. ☐
- I can ask and answer questions with the verb *can*. ☐
- I can make suggestions about what to do. ☐

Get Culture! Kids' London

Hyde Park

The London Eye and the Thames

Natural History Museum

1 **Do you know these places in London? What are they? What can you do there?**

2 **2.49 Listen and read. Match photos A–D to paragraphs 1–4.**

Things to do at the weekend

London is a fun city. There are a lot of things kids can do. Here are some of them.

1 *D* **Go to a museum**
How about the Natural History Museum? There are fun activities for kids: you can make dinosaur T-shirts, see a puppet show or be a scientist for a day!

2 ☐ **Family workshops**
Some museums have family workshops. Mums, dads and their kids can draw, paint or make things together. At the Cartoon Museum you can make your own comic!

3 ☐ **See a show**
London is famous for its musicals. There are many shows for all the family. You can sing and dance to the songs too.

4 ☐ **See the city**
You can see London from the top of the London Eye, or from a boat on the Thames. You can run, play football, skateboard or have a picnic in Hyde Park.

3 **Read the text again. Circle the correct answer.**

Where can you …

1 skateboard?
in the London Eye capsules / in Hyde Park

3 make a comic?
at a workshop / on the Thames

2 sing?
in the Natural History Museum / in a musical

4 go on a boat?
from the top of the London Eye / on the Thames

5 make a T-shirt?
at the Natural History Museum / at the Cartoon Museum

4 **2.50 Listen and write where the people are. Choose from the places in the box.**

A puppet show. A drawing workshop. ~~The London Eye.~~ A musical.

1	*The London Eye.*
2	
3	
4	

5 **Work in pairs. What can kids do where you live? Make a list and compare with other students' lists. Whose list is the longest?**

Free time activities

A 29 **Watch the video and answer the presenter's questions. Which of these activities is not in the video? Circle the correct answer a, b, c or d.**

a boxing   b skateboarding   c swimming   d ice-skating

B 29 **Watch the video again and circle T (true) or F (false). Use the information from the video, not what you know.**

1 You can ride a BMX bike in Rom Park. T / F
2 You can't ride a scooter in Rom Park. T / F
3 You can climb without a special hat. T / F
4 Boxing isn't a sport. T / F
5 Sports can help you make new friends. T / F

C Discuss in pairs. Which of the sports or activities in the video can you do? Which would you like to do?

PROJECT

- **Work in pairs. Make a leaflet about the fun things visitors can do in your area.**
- **Take photos of the places or find them on the Internet.**
- **Write about places with fun activities for kids and their families. Use these questions to help you.**

  What kind of places are they?
  Where are they?
  What can people do there?
- **Put the photos and text together on the leaflet.**
- **Share your leaflet with the class.**

Fun things to do in ...*

- This is ...
- It is **in/near/next to/at** ...
- You can **play football / skateboard / see a film** there.

* Add the name of the place where you live.

6 My day

Vocabulary I can talk about daily activities.

In this unit

Vocabulary

- Daily activities
- Days of the week
- Months

Grammar

- Present Simple affirmative
- Adverbs of frequency

30–31

6.2 Grammar video

32

6.2 Grammar animation

33

6.3 Grammar animation

34

6.4 Communication video

1 Which of these activities do you do every day?

go to school   have lunch   do (my) homework
watch TV   go to bed

I know that!

2 🔊 **3.1** **Listen and repeat. Which expressions can you find in the pictures on page 70?**

Vocabulary **Daily activities**

do my homework get up go to bed
go to school hang out with my friends
have a shower have breakfast have dinner
have lessons have lunch listen to music
tidy my room watch TV

3 **Circle the correct answer.**

1 *get* / *go* to bed
2 *have* / *get* up
3 *tidy* / *listen to* my room
4 *have* / *go* lessons
5 *watch* / *listen to* music
6 *take* / *watch* TV
7 *do* / *have* my homework
8 *take* / *hang out* with my friends

4 **Complete the expressions with the words in the box.**

lessons dinner a shower breakfast ~~lunch~~

2 ________

1 *lunch*

3 ________

have

4 ________

5 ________

LOOK!

have breakfast/lunch/dinner
have **a** shower
have lesson**s**

5 🔊 **3.2** **Listen and write the activity in your notebook. Use the Vocabulary box to help you.**

1 *watch TV*

6 **Number the activities in the order you do them on a typical day. Read your lists in pairs. Are they the same?**

☐ have dinner
☐ have lessons
☐ go to school
☐ do my homework
1 get up
☐ have breakfast
☐ go to bed
☐ have lunch

7 **Look at the pictures. Write the activity.**

1 *hang out with my friends*

2 ________

3 ________

4 ________

5 ________

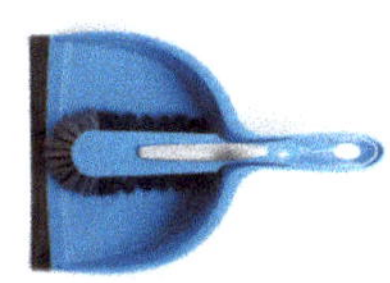

6 ________

8 **In pairs, play the board game on page 70.**

1 Throw a dice.
2 Go forward.
3 If there's a picture on the square, name the activity.
• **Correct answer:** stay there.
• **Wrong answer:** go back two squares.
4 Go to the FINISH first to win!

I remember that!

9 **Put the daily activities in the Vocabulary box into groups.**

:) *My favourite activities: ...*
:(*Activities I don't like: ...*

I listen to classical music

Lucas asks Jen and Alex about their daily routine for a school survey.

1 30 3.3 **Watch or listen and read. Who makes breakfast? Circle the correct answer.**

a Lucas b Alex c Jen

2 Write *A* (Alex), *J* (Jen) or *A and J* (Alex and Jen).

1 get up early *J*
2 make pancakes ____
3 walk to school ____
4 do homework ____
5 listen to classical music ____
6 play the piano ____

3 3.4 **Listen and repeat. Find these expressions in the story.**

Say it!

Me too. Come on, guys! Seriously?

4 Guess! **Circle what you think Alex really does.**

1 gets up *early / late*
2 has breakfast *at home / at school*
3 plays *computer games / football*

5 31 3.5 **Now watch or listen and check.**

Grammar Present Simple affirmative

▶ 32 **Get Grammar!**

	+
I	**listen** to music.
You	**listen** to music.
He/She/It	**listens** to music.
We	**listen** to music.
You	**listen** to music.
They	**listen** to music.

6 **Circle the correct answer.**

I [1](get) / *gets* up early. Alex [2]*get* / *gets* up late. Alex [3]*have* / *has* breakfast at school. I [4]*have* / *has* breakfast at home.

Jen and I [5]*walk* / *walks* to school. After school, we [6]*do* / *does* our homework. In the evening, I [7]*play* / *plays* computer games.

LOOK!

get → gets watch → watches tidy → tidies
make → makes go → goes have → has

7 **Read Lucas's blog. Complete the sentences with a verb in the box in the correct form.**

go hang watch play have
have get ~~get~~

Lucas's blog

My brother and I are very different. Max [1] <u>gets</u> up early. I [2]______ up late. I [3]______ breakfast at home but Max [4]______ to the swimming pool in the morning, so he [5]______ breakfast at school. Before dinner, I [6]______ computer games and Max [7]______ out with his friends. But we [8]______ the football on TV together!

8 **Tick (✔) the things that you do. Tell your partner. Then listen to your partner and tick (✔) the things he/she does.**

	Me	Name: ______
1 I get up early.	☐	☐
2 I get up late.	☐	☐
3 I have breakfast at home.	☐	☐
4 I have breakfast at school.	☐	☐
5 I walk to school.	☐	☐
6 I take the bus to school.	☐	☐
7 I watch TV after dinner.	☐	☐
8 I play computer games after dinner.	☐	☐

9 **Look at Exercise 8. In your notebook, write what you and your partner do.**

I get up early. Nicola gets up early too.
I have breakfast at home. Nicola has …

Fun Spot

10 **Play *Who is it?***

The Terrific Two Dug's busy week

1 Look at the cartoon. Can you see Dug's football shirt? What colour is it?

2 3.6 Listen and read. Which is Dug's free day?

3 You can't see three activities from Dug's busy week in the cartoon. What are they?

4 Correct the sentences.

1 Dug's ~~kitchen~~ is a mess. *garage*
2 Dug has singing lessons. ________
3 Dug has lunch with his Uncle Roberto. ________
4 Dug visits his granny and grandad. ________
5 Dug plays basketball for the superhero team. ________

Grammar Adverbs of frequency

■■■■	We **always** hang out with our friends.
■■■□	He **usually** goes to the gym.
■■□□	I **often** visit my grandma.
■□□□	She **sometimes** has dinner with us.
□□□□	They **never** get up late.

Adverb + verb	Adverb + *to be*
I **always** have breakfast.	I am **always** happy.
They **never** get up late.	They are **never** late.

▶ 33 **Get Grammar!**

5 In your notebook, write how often Dug does these activities.

1 has / usually / at home / breakfast / He / .

He usually has breakfast at home.

2 sometimes / computer games / plays / He / .

3 at home on Tuesday / never / is / He / .

4 listens / He / to music / often / .

5 gets up / He / late / always / .

6 In your notebook, write about Kit's sisters, Lulu and Flo. Use the correct form of the verbs.

1 Lulu and Flo / go to the cinema on Friday. (often)
Lulu and Flo often go to the cinema on Friday.

2 Lulu and Flo / hang out with Kit and Dug. (sometimes)

3 Lulu / go to bed early. (usually)

4 Flo / play computer games. (never)

5 They / be late for school. (sometimes)

6 They / do their homework before dinner. (always)

7 🔊 3.7 Listen and repeat.

Vocabulary Days of the week

Monday Tuesday Wednesday Thursday
Friday Saturday Sunday

8 Complete the words. Tell your partner when Kit does these activities. Which day is missing?

1 watch films	F*r i*day
2 get up late	S_ _ _ _day
3 cook dinner	W_ _ _ _ _day
4 tidy her house	S_ _day
5 have a tennis lesson	M_ _day
6 go to the gym	T_ _ _day

Kit watches films on Friday.

9 In your notebook, write sentences that are true for you. When is your free day?

1 always / Monday
I always watch TV on Monday.

2 sometimes / Tuesday

3 often / Thursday

4 usually / Friday

5 never / Saturday

6 always / Sunday

10 Work in pairs. Say one true and one false activity. Can your partner spot the false sentence?

A: *I never get up late. I often cook.*

B: *True, false!*

A: *Correct!*

The film starts at four o'clock

Alex and Lian want to go to the cinema.

1

Lian: What time is it?
Alex: It's **quarter to four**. (1)
Lian: What time is the film?
Alex: It's at **four o'clock**. (2)
Lian: It's too late now.
Alex: Wait, the film is on again at **half past four**. (3)
Lian: That's better. Let's go.

At the cinema …

2

Lian: There isn't a film at half past four.
Alex: But it says here there is a film at half past four on Fridays. Oh!
Lian: Exactly! Today's Saturday.

1 Find the times (1–3) in the dialogue. Match them with the clocks (a–c).

a ☐  b ☐  c ☐ 

2 ▶34 🔊 3.8 Watch or listen and read. Why isn't there a show at half past four?

3 🔊 3.9 Listen and repeat.

Communication Telling the time

A: What time is it?
B: It's  *four* o'clock.

A: What time is the *film/match*?
B: It's at  *ten* (minutes) past *four*.
 quarter past *four*.
 half past *four*.
 quarter to *five*.
 *ten* (minutes) to *five*.

4 Complete the times. Then ask and answer in pairs.

1 05:40 It's twenty *to* six.
2 02:30 It's ______ past two.
3 10:15 It's quarter ______ ten.
4 03:00 It's three ______ .
5 05:10 It's ten past ______ .
6 07:45 It's quarter ______ eight.

A: *What time is it?* B: *It's twenty to six.*

5 In pairs, make dialogues like those in Exercise 4. Then act them out in class.

1 A: time / the football match? B: 12:15
What time is the football match?
B: time / now? B: 11:55

2 A: time? B: 5:40
B: the party? B: 6:00

Fun Spot

6 Play *What time is it?* as a class. Ask and answer.

A: *What time is it?*
B: *It's one o'clock. What time is it?*
C: *It's five past one. What time is it?*
D: *It's …*

1 Look at the photos and read the first part of the text. Why is this family special?

2 3.10 Read and listen to the text. Circle the correct answer.

1 Réka lives in *Australia* / *different countries*.
2 Réka has got a *brother* / *sister*.
3 Réka *has got* / *hasn't got* a school.
4 Réka hangs out with her friends *in different places* / *online*.
5 *Dreamtime Traveler* is Réka's *book* / *blog*.
6 Réka's life *is* / *isn't* boring.

3 Read the text again and answer the questions.

1 Who is Lalika? *He's Réka's brother.*
2 Who are Réka's teachers?
3 Has Réka got a best friend?
4 What are her two favourite activities?
5 Réka hasn't got a pet. Why?
6 What does Réka watch?

4 What do you like most about Réka's life? Tell a partner.

5 3.11 Listen and repeat. Find the months in the photos.

Vocabulary Months

January February March
April May June
July August September
October November December

6 Imagine you travel to different countries like Réka. Plan your journey for a year. Tell the other students about your plan.

Month	Country
January and February	*Australia*

In January and February I'm in Australia. In March, I'm in …

A day with … *Dreamtime Traveler*!

Australia – January 2016

Réka Kaponay is from Australia, but she lives in different countries! She travels with her parents and brother, Lalika. Today she tells us about her life.

Where's your school?
I haven't got a school! My teachers are my parents and the people we visit.
Who are your friends?
I've got friends in a lot of countries. We hang out online. I haven't got a best friend.
Have you got a pet?
No! I love animals but I can't have a pet. We are always in different places.
What are your favourite hobbies?
Reading and writing! I read a lot and I write my own books. I've got a blog too – *Dreamtime Traveler*. But I also watch TV and films like all teenagers and I love walking and swimming.
Do you like your life?
Yes, I love every day! It's never boring!

Machu Picchu, Peru – March 2013

Nazca, Peru – March 2013

Cappadocia, Turkey – October 2014

Paris, France – August 2015

6.6 Listening and Writing

I can understand and write short texts about a typical weekend.

1 **Tick (✔) the activities you do at the weekend. Compare with your partner.**

1 ☐ tidy my room
2 ☐ play football
3 ☐ ride a horse
4 ☐ listen to music
5 ☐ watch TV
6 ☐ sing
7 ☐ play computer games
8 ☐ do my homework
9 ☐ have lunch with my family

2 **Exam Spot** 🔊 **3.12** **What is their typical Saturday? Listen and match the names to the pictures. There is one extra picture.**

1

2

Brian Ben Anna

3

4

3 🔊 **3.13** **Listen to Ben talking about his weekend. Complete the sentences with the words in the box.**

always	room	~~usually~~	guitar	bed

1 Ben *usually* gets up at 7 o'clock on Saturday.
2 Ben tidies his ______ after breakfast.
3 Ben goes to ______ at 10 o'clock on Saturday.
4 Ben ______ does his homework after breakfast on Sunday.
5 Ben and his best friend play the ______ on Sunday.

4 **Work in groups. Talk about what you usually do at the weekend. Then tell your class about a student in your group. They guess who it is!**

5 **Read Lian's blog. Which is her favourite day? Circle the correct answer.**

a Saturday b Sunday

My weekend

I usually get up at 8 o'clock on Saturdays. After breakfast I skateboard with my friends. I love my skateboard and I love Saturdays! Before dinner I watch TV or play computer games.

I get up at 9 o'clock on Sundays. Before lunch I tidy my room and I do my homework. I always have lunch with my family! After lunch I often draw or listen to music.

Writing *before, after*

lunch

tidy my room —— lunch —— play computer games

Before lunch I tidy my room.
I tidy my room before lunch.

After lunch I play computer games.
I play computer games after lunch.

6 **Underline *before* and *after* in Lian's blog.**

7 **Writing Time** **Write about your typical weekend. Use *before* and *after*.**

Find ideas

Make a list of what you do.
Saturday: get up late, help Mum, …
Sunday: do my homework, …

Draft

1 Write a paragraph about Saturday.
I usually get up at … o'clock on Saturday. I have a shower and I have breakfast. After breakfast I …
2 Write a paragraph about Sunday.
I always … on Sunday. Before lunch I …

Check and write

Check all *before* and *after* and write the final version of your text.

Vocabulary

1 Complete the expressions with words in the box. There's one extra word.

go to · watch · ~~homework~~ · listen to · up · have · my room · friends · school

1 do my *homework*
2 get ______
3 ______ TV
4 go to ______
5 ______ bed
6 ______ music
7 tidy ______
8 hang out with ______

The extra word is ______ .

2 Write three collocations with the extra word in Exercise 1. Do you know any more collocations with this word?

1 ______ a sh_ _ _r
2 ______ b_ _ _k_ _ _t
3 ______ le_ _on_

3 Find and circle the days of the week. Say them in the correct order with your partner. Which day is missing?

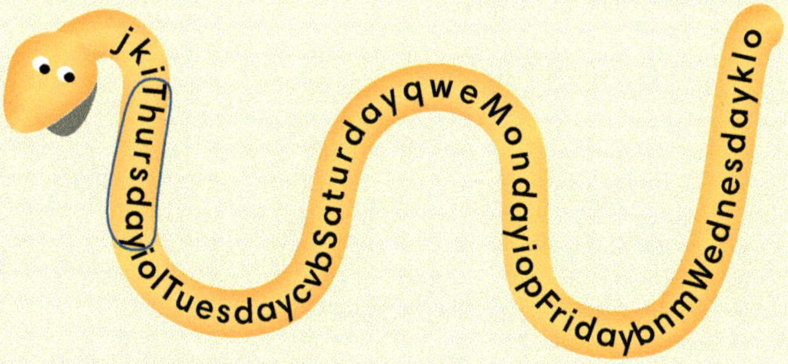

4 Answer the questions. Then tell a friend.

1 What month is your birthday? ______
2 What month is Christmas? ______
3 What month is after February? ______
4 What month is before August? ______

Pronunciation

5 3.14 Listen and repeat: /s/, /z/ or /ɪz/?

Kate gets up late and has breakfast fast,
She watches a film and runs for the bus!

Grammar

6 Complete Carla's blog about her typical morning. Use the verbs in the box in the correct form.

go · get (x3) · hang · have (x3) · listen

I [1] *get* up at half past seven but my parents [2]______ up at seven o'clock. My sister, Kate, [3]______ up late every day! We [4]______ breakfast together. After breakfast I [5]______ to school with Kate. We go on the bus. Kate [6]______ to music and I [7]______ out with my friends. We [8]______ lessons and we [9]______ lunch at one o'clock.

7 In your notebook, write sentences that are true for you.

1 My brother / sister (always)
My brother always gets up late.
2 My parents (usually)
3 My best friend (often)
4 My granny and grandad (sometimes)
5 My teacher (never)
6 I (always)

Communication

8 Match 1–3 to a–c and make two dialogues.

Dialogue 1

1 [b] What time is it?
2 [ ] What time is the show?
3 [ ] Let's watch it.

a OK!
b It's five to two.
c At two o'clock.

Dialogue 2

1 [ ] When is the match?
2 [ ] What time is it now?
3 [ ] Let's walk fast then!

a It's ten to six.
b Yes, let's go!
c It's at six o'clock.

Check yourself! ✓

- I can talk about daily activities. [ ]
- I can use the Present Simple in affirmative sentences. [ ]
- I can use adverbs of frequency. [ ]
- I can tell the time. [ ]

Reading and Writing

1 **Work in pairs. Tell a partner what you and your family can and can't do.**

A: *I can play the guitar.*

B: *My granny can't use a mobile phone!*

2 **Exam Spot** **Read the ad. What is it about? Circle the correct answer.**

a A talent contest. b A London show.

3 **Read the ad again. Answer the questions.**

1 Who is Meryl? *She's a new star.*
2 What can she do?
3 How many prizes are there?
4 When is the contest?
5 Where is it?
6 Can dogs come?

'NEW STARS!'
You can be a star too!

This is Meryl. She's a new star! She sings and plays the guitar in a rock band. She can dance too.

What can you do? Show us! We've got special prizes.

Prize 1 You can be on TV!
Prize 2 Meet a famous band!
Prize 3 Go to a London show!

When: Saturday at 10 o'clock
Where: Town Theatre
Your family and friends can come too!
We're sorry but no cats or dogs.

4 **Exam Spot** **Complete Dan's blog with words in the box. There are two extra words.**

can After hang the get listen garden room usually breakfast have ~~house~~

I'm at my cousin Julie's [1]*house* this week. It's in the country. It isn't very big but it's got a fantastic [2]_______ ! My uncle and aunt [3]_______ up at half past six. I get up and have [4]_______ with them and Julie. [5]_______ breakfast I go to bed again – it's the holidays! Then I tidy my [6]_______ . Julie and I [7]_______ do sports after lunch. Julie [8]_______ skateboard really well. She's my new teacher! We often [9]_______ out with Julie's friends before dinner. Before bed we [10]_______ to music or watch TV.

5 **Exam Spot** **You are at a friend's house for the holidays. Write 40–50 words about what you do. Use these questions to help you.**

1 Where is your friend's house?
2 What time do you get up?
3 What do you do before and after lunch?
4 What do you do in the evening?

I'm at my friend's house in (the) …
I get up at … I have breakfast with …
Before lunch I … After lunch we …
In the evening we …

Listening

6 **Exam Spot** 3.15 **Listen and tick (✔) the correct answer.**

1 What can Grace do?

a ☐  b ☑  c ☐ 

2 What club is on Thursdays?

a ☐  b ☐  c ☐ 

3 What time is the film?

a ☐ 

b ☐ 

c ☐ 

4 Where is Jill?

a ☐  b ☐  c ☐ 

5 What can Uncle Jack do?

a ☐  b ☐  c ☐ 

Communication

7 Exam Spot **Look at the pictures. Match a–h to 1–6. There are two extra sentences.**

a No, it's not a good idea.
b The film's at quarter to five.
c Let's do something fun!
d Let's go skateboarding!
e Swimming? I'm not sure.
f Swimming? Great idea!
g We can ride our bikes!
h What time is it?

8 Exam Spot **Work in pairs. Ask and answer the questions.**

1 What's your favourite month?
2 Who can sing in your family?
3 What cool things can you do?
4 Have you got a book in English?

Exam Language Bank

Action verbs

act	dive	fly	ride	skateboard
climb	draw	jump	run	swim
cook	fix	read	sing	write

make, play, ride

make a poster
cupcakes
play computer games
football
the piano
ride a bike
a horse

Days of the week

Monday
Tuesday
Wednesday
Thursday
Friday
Saturday
Sunday

Daily activities

do my homework
get up
go to bed
go to school
have lessons
hang out with my friends
have a shower
have breakfast
have dinner
have lunch
listen to music
tidy my room
watch TV

Months

January
February
March
April
May
June
July
August
September
October
November
December

Suggestions

Let's *do something fun*!
Let's *go ice-skating*!
We can *go to the park*.

I agree!
Let's do that!
Great idea!
I'm not sure.
It's not a good idea.

Telling the time

What time is it?
It's *four* o'clock.

What time is the *film*/*match*?
It's at *ten* (minutes) past *four*.
It's at quarter past *four*.
It's at half past *four*.
It's at quarter to *five*.
It's at *ten* (minutes) to *five*.

7 Animals

Vocabulary I can talk about animals.

In this unit

Vocabulary
- Wild animals
- Pets
- Money
- Adjectives

Grammar
- Present Simple negative, questions and short answers

35-36

7.2 Grammar video

37

7.2 Grammar animation

38

7.3 Grammar animation

39

7.4 Communication video

40

BBC Culture video

I know that!

1 Find the animals in the photos. There is one extra photo.

elephant monkey tiger giraffe lion crocodile kangaroo

2 3.16 Listen and repeat. What is the name of the animal in the extra photo on page 82?

Vocabulary Wild animals

bird butterfly crocodile elephant fish fly frog giraffe kangaroo lion monkey snake spider tiger whale

3 Look at the pictures and complete the words. Use the Vocabulary box to help you.

1 

bu *t* *t* er *f* ly

2 

b _ r _

3 

_ ly

4 

s _ ak _

5 

_ pid _ _

6 

f _ _ g

7 

_ is _

4 3.17 Listen to the animal sounds. Number the words. Then check your answers in pairs.

a ☐ bird
b ☐ elephant
c ☐ frog
d *1* lion
e ☐ monkey
f ☐ snake

5 Read the sentences and circle the correct answer.

1 I can fly! — spider / (bird)
2 I can swim! — whale / butterfly
3 I'm very tall! — frog / giraffe
4 I can't jump! — kangaroo / elephant
5 I've got big teeth! — crocodile / fly
6 I've got arms and legs. — snake / monkey

6 The names of the animals got mixed. Write the correct names.

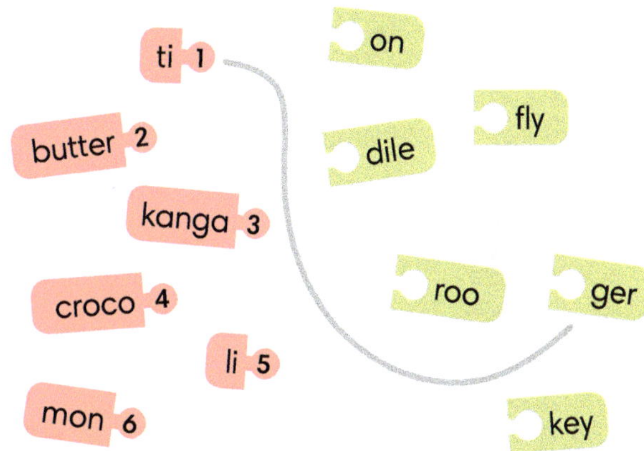

1 *tiger*
2 ______
3 ______
4 ______
5 ______
6 ______

I remember that!

7 Work in pairs. Draw three fantasy animals. Show them to your partner to give them a name.

A: *It's a giraffe and a bird.*
B: *It's a 'giraffird'!*

7.2 Grammar

I can use the negative form of the Present Simple and talk about pets.

I don't like cats!

1

Alex: Mum? I want a dog like this! Please?
Mum: Aww … I like dogs but they are hard work, Alex.
Alex: I don't mind!

2

Mum: Can you get up early and take it for a walk? Every day?
Jen: Poor dog! Alex doesn't get up before twelve o'clock at the weekend.
Dad: Big dogs eat a lot.
Alex: But it's small! It doesn't eat a lot.
Dad: Because it's a puppy! These dogs are usually very big!
Alex: Oh, all right.

3

Jen: How about a cat? People don't take cats for a walk.
Alex: I don't like cats! And I'm allergic!
Dad: Look, these are perfect for you! They don't eat a lot and you are not allergic to them.

1 35 3.18 **Watch or listen and read. Find a word that means 'baby dog'.**

2 Read the sentences. Circle T (true) or F (false).

1 Alex wants a pet cat. T / (F)
2 Dad thinks small dogs eat a lot. T / F
3 Alex gets up late at the weekend. T / F
4 The puppy in Alex's photo is very big. T / F
5 A cat is not a good pet for Alex. T / F

3 3.19 **Listen and repeat. Find these expressions in the story.**

Say it!

I don't mind! Poor (dog)! Oh, all right.

4 Guess! **What kind of pet is good for Alex in Dad's opinion? Have a class vote.**

a hamster **b** goldfish **c** frog

5 36 3.20 **Now watch or listen and check.**

Grammar Present Simple negative

I **don't (do not)** get up early.
You **don't (do not)** get up early.
He/She/It **doesn't (does not)** get up early.
We **don't (do not)** get up early.
You **don't (do not)** get up early.
They **don't (do not)** get up early.

6 Circle the correct answer. Then check with the story on page 84.

1 Alex *wants* / *doesn't want* a cat. (*doesn't want* circled)
2 Alex says small dogs *eat* / *don't eat* a lot.
3 Alex's mum *likes* / *doesn't like* the puppy in the photo.
4 Alex *gets up* / *doesn't get up* before twelve o'clock at the weekend.
5 People *take* / *don't take* cats for a walk.

7 Complete what Alex says with *don't* or *doesn't*.

1 On weekdays Jen and I go to school but we *don't* go to school at the weekend.

2 At the weekend Lucas plays computer games but he ________ play computer games on weekdays.

3 On weekdays Jen gets up early but she ________ get up early at the weekend.

4 I hang out with my friends at the weekend but I ________ hang out with them on weekdays.

5 On weekdays Lian does homework but she ________ do homework at the weekend.

6 At the weekend my family and I go out for lunch but we ________ go out for lunch on weekdays.

8 In pairs, talk about what you do and don't do at the weekend.

I don't go to school at the weekend.

9 🔊 3.21 Listen and repeat. Then label the pictures with the words in the Vocabulary box.

Vocabulary Pets

cat dog goldfish hamster iguana
parrot rabbit tortoise

1 *cat* 2 ________ 3 ________ 4 ________

5 ________ 6 ________ 7 ________ 8 ________

10 Which pet is good for these people?
Student B: Go to page 108 to help Student A.
Student A: Listen to Student B and decide which pet is good for them.

1 **Alex:** *goldfish* / *dog*? (*dog* circled)
2 **Lucas:** *parrot* / *hamster*?
3 **Lian:** *iguana* / *rabbit*?

B: *Alex wants to play with his pet.*
A: *A dog is a good pet for Alex.*

Student A: Go to page 106 to help Student B.
Student B: Listen to student A and decide which pet is good for them.

4 **Granny:** *dog* / *hamster*?
5 **Aunt Megan:** *tortoise* / *parrot*?
6 **Jen's friend, Emma:** *goldfish* / *big dog*?

The Terrific Two Superdug's interview

1 **Look at the cartoon. What magazine is Kit reading?**

2 3.22 **Listen and read. Who is Superdug's piano teacher?**

3 **Read the sentences. Circle the correct answer.**

1 Superdug *watches TV* / *plays computer games* to relax.
2 Superdug *sometimes* / *always* wins a computer game.
3 Kit *speaks* / *doesn't speak* foreign languages.
4 Superdug *is* / *isn't* a good piano player.
5 Kit *sings* / *doesn't sing* well.

Grammar
Present Simple questions and short answers

▶ 38 **Get Grammar!**

?	Short answers
Do I **sing**?	Yes, I **do**. / No, I **don't**.
Do you **sing**?	Yes, you **do**. / No, you **don't**.
Does he/she/it **sing**?	Yes, he/she/it **does**. / No, he/she/it **doesn't**.
Do we **sing**?	Yes, we **do**. / No, we **don't**.
Do you **sing**?	Yes, you **do**. / No, you **don't**.
Do they **sing**?	Yes, they **do**. / No, they **don't**.
What **do** you **do** to relax?	I play computer games.

4 Complete the reporter's questions to Superdug with *Do* or *Does*.

1 *Do* you know Superman? ✗
2 ______ you hang out with friends? ✓
3 ______ Kit help you? ✓
4 ______ you go to the gym? ✓
5 ______ you and Kit listen to music? ✗
6 ______ Kit visit you at the weekend? ✗

5 In your notebook, write Superdug's answers to the questions in Exercise 4.

1 ✗ *No, I don't.*

6 In pairs, roleplay the questions and answers in Exercises 4 and 5.

A: *Do you know Superman?*
B: *No, I don't.*

7 In your notebook, write the questions to Kit.

1 you / play the guitar?
Do you play the guitar?
2 you / listen to pop music?
3 Superdug / eat superhero food?
4 Superdug / watch TV?
5 you and Superdug / hang out every day?
6 Superdug / have swimming lessons?

8 3.23 Listen to Kit's answers to the questions in Exercise 7. Write them in your notebook.

1 *No, I don't.*

9 Game! Complete the questions. In pairs, ask the questions and mime the answers. Get a point for each correct guess.

1 What *do you do* (do) to relax?
2 What ______ (have) for breakfast?
3 Where ______ (do) your homework?
4 What ______ (do) after school?
5 What ______ (do) on Friday after dinner?
6 Where ______ (hang out) with your friends?

A: *What do you do to relax?*
B: (mimes the answer)
A: *I know! You play the guitar!*

10 3.24 3.25
Go to page 107.
Listen and sing the Questions Song.

7.4 Communication I can buy a ticket.

One ticket, please

Dad:	Get a ticket, Lucas. Jen and I have got passes.
Attendant:	Can I help you?
Lucas:	Can I have a ticket to the zoo, please?
Attendant:	That's eighteen pounds fifty, please.
Lucas:	Here you are.
Attendant:	Thank you. Here's your ticket. Would you like a guide?
Lucas:	No, thank you. Just the ticket, please. I've got all the information on my phone.
Lucas:	Where do we start?
Jen:	At the café. I'm so hungry I could eat a horse!
Lucas:	Shh! We are at the zoo.

1 39 3.26 **Watch or listen and read. Why don't they need a guide?**

2 3.27 **Listen and repeat.**

Communication Buying a ticket

A: Can I help you?
B: Can I have *one ticket* / *two tickets* to the *zoo*, please?
A: That's *eighteen pounds fifty*.
B: Here you are.
A: Here's your ticket. / Here are your tickets.
B: Thanks.

3 3.28 **Put the sentences in the dialogue in the correct order. Then listen and check.**

a ☐ Thanks.
b ☐ Here are your tickets.
c ☐ Can I have three tickets to the aquarium, please?
d ☐ Here you are.
e ☐ That's twelve pounds sixty, please.
f [1] Can I help you?

LOOK! £ = pound
£4.20 = four (pounds) twenty

4 Write how much it is.

1 *eighteen pounds fifty*

2 ______

3 ______

4 ______

5 In pairs, roleplay buying a ticket to the museum. Use the prompts.

A: help / you? *Can I help you?*	B: three tickets
A: £ 24.60	B: here
A: your tickets	B: thanks

6 In pairs, act out three more dialogues. Use the tickets in Exercise 4 and the expressions in the Communication box.

1 In your notebook, write names of animals which …

a swim very well. **b** eat a lot. **c** can sing.

2 **Exam Spot** 3.29 Read and listen to the web page about amazing animals. Match texts 1–3 to photos A–C.

Amazing animals!

A

an elephant

B

a giraffe

C

a humpback whale

1 ☐ These animals are very fast. They can run at 55 kilometres an hour! They only sleep one or two hours every night. They've got cute faces. They don't drink much water but they like eating. They can eat leaves from tall trees. They eat 45 kilos of food every day!

2 ☐ These animals are big but they can run very fast. They love water and they can swim too. They love their families. They are very clever and friendly but sometimes they can be dangerous! They eat plants. They eat up to 270 kilos of food and they drink about 75 litres of water every day!

3 ☐ These animals eat a lot of very small fish and are very strong. They can jump out of the water. They like having fun! We can't hear them but they sing and they 'write' songs! Some people think they are ugly but in fact they are cute.

3 Read the text again and complete the table.

	giraffes	elephants	humpback whales
What do they eat/drink?	*leaves, …*		
What can they do?			*jump, …*
What do they like/love?			

4 3.30 Listen and repeat. Then label pictures 1–6 with the adjectives in the Vocabulary box.

Vocabulary Adjectives

cute dangerous fast slow strong ugly

1 *dangerous*

2 ________

3 ________

4 ________

5 ________

6 ________

5 Read the text again. Find and underline adjectives used to describe each animal.

6 3.31 Listen to two children. Write the animals they speak about.

Speaker 1: ________

Speaker 2: ________

Fun Spot

7 Game! Work in teams of four. Your teacher says an adjective. Write as many animals with that quality as you can in one minute. Compare your animals with other teams.

Teacher: *fast*

Team: *giraffe, elephant, …*

7.6 Listening and Writing

I can understand and write short texts about pets.

1 **In pairs, make a list of animals that you can find in pet shops. Then underline animals that are easy to look after in your opinion.**

Cats – easy. They don't go for a walk!

2 **3.32** **Listen to a radio interview with Jo. She's got a pet shop. Tick (✔) the animals on your list that you hear.**

3 **Exam Spot** **3.32** **Listen again. Look and tick (✔) a, b or c.**

1 Which animal is dangerous?

a ☐ 

b ☐ 

c ☐ 

2 What do dogs like?

a ☐ 

b ☐ 

c ☐ 

3 Which pet is easy to look after?

a ☐ 

b ☐ 

c ☐ 

4 **3.33** **Listen to George talking about his new pet. Circle the correct answers.**

1 George's rabbit is *(clever)* / *boring*.
2 His favourite place is *his rabbit house* / *the garden*.
3 He eats *green* / *red and green* vegetables.
4 He drinks *water* / *milk*.
5 George has got *one rabbit* / *two rabbits*.

5 **What's your ideal pet? What do you know about it? Tell a partner.**

6 **Read Martin's email to Jen. Is it about …**

a his weekend? **b** his puppy?

Hi Jen,
Can you look after my puppy for the weekend? His name's Rex.
He eats dog food and he drinks water. He likes milk too. He goes for a walk after his breakfast and dinner. He sleeps a lot. He's very friendly and very cute! Is this OK? Let me know.
Martin

Writing Starting and ending an email

Begin with *Hi* / *Hello*.
Write a comma after the name, e.g. *Hi Jen, …*
Write your name at the end, e.g. *Martin*.

7 **Put the sentences in order to make an email.**

a ☐ She eats cat food and fish. She drinks wat
b ☐ Helena
c ☐ Is this OK? Let me know.
d *1* Hi Ben,
e ☐ Can you look after my cat for the weekenc

8 **Writing Time** **Write an email to a friend. Ask him/her to look after your pet.**

Find ideas

Make notes about your pet.
Decide which friend you're writing to.

Draft

1 Write *Hi/Hello* and your friend's name.
2 Explain why you are writing.
Can you look after my … for the weekend?
3 Give helpful information.
He/She eats/drinks/likes/sleeps …
He/She is very … and …
4 End your note.
Is this OK? Let me know.
5 Write your name.

Check and write

Check the beginning and ending of your email. Write the final version of your text.

Vocabulary

1 Circle the odd one out. Why is it different?

1 a bird	b butterfly	c fly	(d) kangaroo
2 a crocodile	b snake	c tiger	d elephant
3 a monkey	b fish	c frog	d whale
4 a giraffe	b lion	c spider	d tiger

2 Write how many of these pets you can see.

1 cats *one*	4 goldfish ____	7 dogs ____
2 rabbits ____	5 tortoises ____	8 hamsters ____
3 parrots ____	6 iguanas ____	

3 Complete the adjectives.

1 strong	3 danger _ _ _	5 fa _ _
2 sl _ _	4 ug _ _	6 cu _ _

Pronunciation

4 3.34 Listen and repeat: /s/.

Sue's snake Simon just eats, eats and eats.

He sits on the sofa and steals all the sweets!

Grammar

5 Read the text and write negative sentences in your notebook.

> **Jason and his family are very different!**
>
> Jason wants an iguana. His sister, Jackie, wants a rabbit and their parents want a parrot!
>
> They all watch TV. Jackie and their parents like films and Jason likes cartoons!
>
> At the weekends Jason goes to the park with his friends, Jackie hangs out with her best friend and their parents visit the neighbours.

1 Jackie and Jason / want / a parrot
Jackie and Jason don't want a parrot.
2 Their parents / want / an iguana
3 Jackie / like / cartoons
4 Jason / go to the park / with parents
5 Their parents / go to / the park

6 In your notebook, write questions and short answers.

1 Jason / want /a rabbit
A: *Does Jason want a rabbit?*
B: *No, he doesn't.*
2 their parents / want / an iguana?
3 they all / watch TV?
4 What / Jackie / do / at the weekend?
5 Where / Jason / go / at the weekend?

Communication

7 Read the mini-dialogues and circle a or b.

1 Can I help you?
a Can I have a ticket, please?
b Would you like a ticket?
2 That's ten pounds ninety.
a The money's here. b Here you are.
3 Here are your tickets.
a Thanks. b No, they aren't.

Check yourself!

- I can talk about pets. ☐
- I can use the negative form of the Present Simple ☐
- I can ask questions in the Present Simple. ☐
- I can buy a ticket. ☐

Get Culture! Pets in the UK

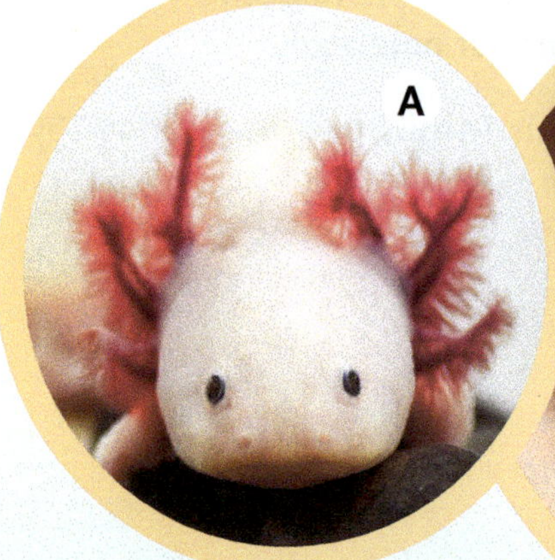

1 Discuss these questions in class.

1 Which pets are popular in your country?
2 Do you know any unusual pets? What are they?
3 Would you like to have an exotic animal as a pet?

2 3.35 Listen and read. Match photos A–D to texts 1–3. There is one extra photo.

Pets in the UK

Some people in the UK want an unusual pet. This is why they choose exotic animals. Here are three unusual pets that you can have in the UK.

1 ☐ Tarantulas

Spiders are scary but some people think tarantulas are pretty. They are quiet animals and they don't need a lot of space or food, so they aren't hard work.

2 ☐ Pygmy hedgehogs

People like pygmy hedgehogs because they are small and cute. They eat cat food and they eat a lot! This is why they need a lot of space to run and play.

3 ☐ Axolotls

They've got a funny name and they look funny too. They live in the water. They can be brown, black, yellow, white or other colours. And here's an amazing fact: if they lose a part of their body, they can make a new one!

3 Read the texts again and answer the questions.

1 Which pet eats a lot?
The pygmy hedgehog.
2 Which pet can make new body parts?
3 Which pet needs a lot of space?
4 Which pet doesn't need a lot of food?
5 Which pet can be different colours?
6 Which pet can be scary?

4 3.36 Listen and circle the correct answer.

1 Which is the number one pet in the UK?
a Cats. (b) Dogs.
2 Which animal is number 3 in the list?
a Rabbit. b Fish.
3 Which are two top names for pets in the UK?
a Alfie and Bella. b Cookie and Dolly.
4 What's their dog's name?
a George. b Mrs C.

5 Work in pairs. Imagine you can have one of the animals in photos A–D.

1 Which of the animals do you choose? Why?
2 Think of a name for your animal.

The London Zoo

BBC

A ▶ 40 **Watch the video and answer the presenter's questions. What do the animals do after breakfast?**

B ▶ 40 **Watch the video again. Write the animals in the box next to the correct sentence. Use the information from the video, not what you know.**

penguins	stick insects	tigers	monkeys	tortoises	lions

1 They're fast. ____________

2 They're slow. ____________

3 They're green. ____________

4 They eat fish. ____________

5 They eat meat. ____________

6 They love toys. ____________

C Discuss in groups. Which animals in the London Zoo would you like to see? Why?

PROJECT

- **Make a class digital photo album of the class pets and/or your ideal pets.**
- **Create a digital poster about your pet and/or your ideal pet. Write short descriptions. Use these questions to help you.**

What are they?	What do they eat?
What are their names?	What can they do?
What do they look like?	What is a fun fact about them?

- **Add photos to your descriptions.**
- **Collect all the posters to make a digital class album.**

8 I like that!

Vocabulary I can talk about sports.

In this unit

Vocabulary
- Sports
- Seasons and weather
- Healthy lifestyle

Grammar
- *love/like/don't like/hate + -ing*
- Object pronouns
- Question words

41–42

8.2 Grammar video

43

8.2 Grammar animation

44

8.3 Grammar animation

45

8.4 Communication video

1 Read these words. What do they mean?

tennis football volleyball basketball swimming skateboarding

I know that!

2 3.37 **Listen and repeat. Find the sports in the photos on page 94. One sport appears twice. What is it?**

Vocabulary Sports

badminton basketball cycling
football hockey ice-skating roller skating
sailing skateboarding skiing
swimming table tennis taekwondo
tennis volleyball windsurfing

3 Exam Spot **Write the words. Use the Vocabulary box to help you.**

1 **tekaodnwo** t a e k w o n d o
2 **siilang** s _ _ _ _ _ g
3 **rloerl kasitng** r _ _ _ _ r s _ _ _ _ g
4 **sktbraoadenig** _ _ _ _ _ _ _ _ _ _ _ _ _
5 **siknig** s _ _ _ _ g
6 **hoecky** h _ _ _ _ y
7 **bsktbaelal** b _ _ _ _ _ _ _ _ l
8 **bdatinmon** b _ _ _ _ _ _ _ n

4 Work in pairs. Put the sports in the Vocabulary box in groups. A sport can be in more than one group.

Indoor sports: *basketball,* ______
Outdoor sports: *football,* ______
Team sports: ______
Winter sports: ______
Water sports: ______

LOOK!
I **do** taekwondo.
I **go** swimming.
I **play** tennis.

5 3.38 **Write *go* or *play*. Compare in pairs. Then listen and check.**

1 *go* cycling	7 ______ windsurfing
2 ______ basketball	8 ______ badminton
3 ______ hockey	9 ______ table tennis
4 ______ skiing	10 ______ sailing
5 ______ skateboarding	11 ______ football
6 ______ roller skating	12 ______ ice-skating

6 What sports do they do? Complete the sentences with *do*, *go* and *play* and the words in the box.

badminton hockey roller skating sailing
skiing swimming table tennis taekwondo

Mario

Sue

Peter

Fran

Mario [1]*plays badminton* at school.
He [2]______ at the weekend.
Sue [3]______ at school.
She also [4]______ with her dad.
Peter [5]______.
He [6]______ every week.
Fran [7]______ in winter.
She always [8]______ in the morning.

I remember that!

7 Complete the sentences with the names of sports. Add *do*, *go* or *play* where necessary.

I never ______.
I watch ______ on TV.
I think ______ is boring.
I think ______ is great!
I ______ with friends.
I ______ every day.
I often ______ at school.

Let's go to summer camp!

Lian: Hey guys, do you want to go to summer camp with me?
Alex: Maybe. What do you do there?
Lian: Horse-riding, rock climbing … I like rock climbing.
Jen: I don't like it!
Lian: How about water sports? There's sailing, windsurfing …
Alex: No, thanks. I don't like getting wet.
Jen: That's true. Lian, you like sports. We like them, but we want to do other things too. Cooking, for example?
Lian: There's a cooking camp in …
Alex: No, thanks. I love eating but I hate cooking!
Lian: Let's find a camp we all like.

1 41 3.39 **Watch or listen and read. Find two sports in the dialogue that are not in the Vocabulary box on p. 95.**

2 Read the dialogue again. Complete the sentences with one word.

1 Lian wants to go to *summer* camp.
2 ________ doesn't like rock climbing.
3 Sailing and windsurfing are ________ sports.
4 Windsurfing is not a good sport for ________ .
5 Jen wants to go to a ________ camp but Alex doesn't.

3 3.40 **Listen and repeat. Find these expressions in the dialogue.**

Say it!

Maybe. That's true.

4 Guess! **Look at the summer camp brochures. Which camp is good for all three of them? Circle a, b or c.**

a tech camp **b** fun camp **c** sports camp

5 42 3.41 **Now watch or listen and check.**

Grammar
love/like/don't like/hate + -ing

I **love** eating.
I **don't like** getting wet.
I **hate** cooking.

Do you **like** cycl**ing**? Yes, I do. / No, I don't.

What **do** you **like** do**ing**? I **like** cook**ing**.

▶43 **Get Grammar!**

6 **Read the dialogue on page 96 again. Complete the sentences with *likes*, *doesn't like*, *loves* or *hates*.**

1 Jen *doesn't like* rock climbing.
2 Lian ________ rock climbing.
3 Alex ________ getting wet.
4 Alex ________ eating but he ________ cooking.

7 **Look at the photos. Write true sentences in your notebook. Use *love*, *like*, *don't like* or *hate* + *-ing*.**

get up draw play swim
cook do homework

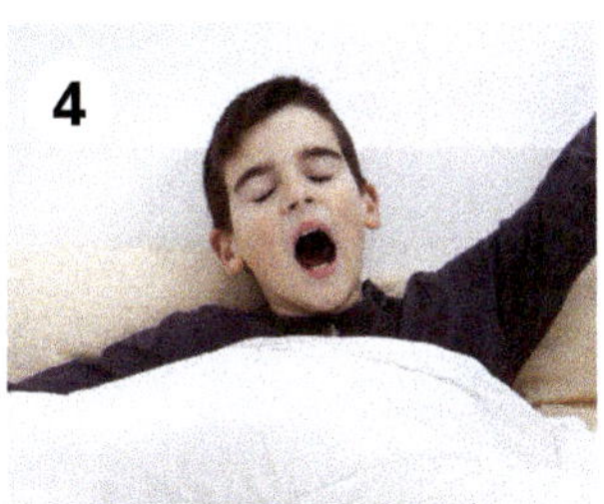

1 *I like playing computer games.*

8 3.42 **What do these people like or don't like doing? Listen and circle T (true) or F (false).**

1	She doesn't like playing volleyball.	T / (F)
2	Brian likes swimming.	T / F
3	She hates getting up early.	T / F
4	They love skateboarding.	T / F
5	Jake doesn't like playing football.	T / F

Grammar Object pronouns

I → **me**	he → **him**	we → **us**
you → **you**	she → **her**	you → **you**
	it → **it**	they → **them**

She is a good friend. I like **her**.
You don't like **sports**. We love **them**.

9 **Read Lian's email. Circle the correct answer.**

My friend, Alex, loves fixing computers. [1](He) / *Him* knows a lot of things about [2]*they* / *them*. I don't, so I usually ask [3]*he* / *him* for help. [4]*We* / *Us* often hang out with his sister, Jen. I like [5]*she* / *her* a lot. Jen loves making cupcakes. [6]*They* / *Them* are amazing! Alex and I love chocolate so [7]*she* / *her* often makes chocolate cupcakes for [8]*we* / *us*.

10 **Write about your friends or family. What do they *love/like/don't like/hate doing*? Use Lian's email in Exercise 9 to help you.**

My friend, …, likes … He/She knows a lot of things about …

8.3 Grammar I can ask detailed questions.

The Terrific Two Dug's sports hero

1 Look at the cartoon. Who has got a mobile phone in the story?

2 3.43 Listen and read. Who is Irina Peters?

3 Read the sentences. Circle T (true) or F (false).

1 Irina wants Dug's autograph. T / (F)
2 Irina is Superdug's fan. T / F
3 Kit doesn't know who Irina Peters is. T / F
4 Dug's got the wrong phone. T / F
5 Dug doesn't know where his phone is. T / F

Grammar Question words

Who is Dug's sports hero?	It's Irina Peters.
What have you got there?	I've got Irina's autograph.
When is the game?	It's on Tuesday.
Where does she live?	She lives in London.
Whose phone is it?	It's Irina's phone.
How many photos have you got?	I've got 80 photos.

▶ 44 Get Grammar!

4 Match the questions to the answers.

1 [d] Where do Superdug and Kit live?
2 [ ] Who is a tennis champion?
3 [ ] How many sisters has Kit got?
4 [ ] When is Dug's birthday?
5 [ ] What is Kit's favourite dinner?
6 [ ] Whose bike is red and white?

a Two.
b Fish and chips.
c Irina.
d In the UK.
e Superdug's.
f On 5th July.

5 Do you know the Teffific Two? Write questions in your notebook. Then answer the questions in pairs.

1 (look at page 14)
A: *Who is uncle Roberto?*
B: *He's Superdug's uncle.*
2 (look at page 26)
3 (look at page 38)
4 (look at page 50)
5 (look at page 62)
6 (look at page 74)

6 3.44 Listen to Superdug's questions. Then circle Kit's answers.

1 (On Wednesdays.) / At her house.
2 Two cars. / I've got them.
3 In Spain. / You are.
4 It's my sister's. / Two sisters.
5 They're Wonder Will's. / I think there are four.
6 It's in your room. / It's nice.

7 Exam Spot Write questions about the underlined sentence fragments.

1 A: *What is your favourite sport* ?
B: My favourite sport is rock climbing.
2 A: ______________________ ?
B: My favourite sportsperson is Andy Murray.
3 A: ______________________ ?
B: I live at 6 Rose Street.
4 A: ______________________ ?
B: My birthday is on August 26.
5 A: ______________________ ?
B: This is my phone.
6 A: ______________________ ?
B: I've got one brother and one sister.

8 In pairs, ask questions in Exercise 7 and give true answers.

A: *What is your favourite sport?*
B: *It's … .*

Fun Spot

9 Game! Make as many questions as you can in three minutes. Use only the words in the box! Who is the winner?

where	Jack	swim	is
does	can	when	what
whose	who	he	like

Where is Jack? Can Jack swim? …

What's the weather like?

Jen: Hi Lucas! Why aren't you at the beach? Isn't it hot and sunny?
Lucas: It's three o'clock. It's too hot and too sunny. What's the weather like in the UK?
Jen: It's cold and rainy. We can't go swimming.
Lucas: That's a pity.
Jen: Yes, but it's OK. It often rains in summer.
Lucas: Well, I hope it's sunny tomorrow.
Jen: Ouch! Me too, but I still can't go swimming.
Lucas: Why?
Jen: I have a dentist's appointment!
Lucas: Eurgh! I hate going to the dentist.
Jen: Me too!
Lucas: See you soon! Bye!

Lucas is on holiday in Spain but it's rainy in London.

1 45 3.45 **Watch or listen and read. Complete the sentence.**

Jen can't go swimming today because ________ .

2 3.46 **Listen and repeat.**

> **Communication**
> **Talking about the weather**
>
> **A:** What's the weather like?
> **B:** It's *cloudy/cold/hot/rainy/snowy/sunny/warm/windy.*
> It's *cold/hot/rainy/sunny* in *winter/summer/autumn/spring.*

3 What's the weather like? Complete the sentences.

1 It's *rainy* .

2 It's ________ .

3 It's ________ .

4 It's ________ .

4 Which months are in each season?

1 Summer: ________
2 Spring: ________
3 Winter: ________
4 Autumn: ________

5 Exam Spot Circle the best answer.

1 A: What's the weather like in autumn in Spain?
B: a It is warm and sunny. b I hope it's warm
c I like sunny weather.

2 A: I want to go windsurfing tomorrow.
B: a Yes, it's cold.
b It's usually warm and windy.
c I hope it's warm and windy.

3 A: What's the weather like today?
B: a It's often cold and cloudy.
b It's cold and cloudy.
c Yes, it is.

Fun Spot

6 Game! Sports and weather.
Student A: Say what the weather is like.
Student B: Suggest a sport you can do.
Then swap roles.

A: *It's windy.* **B:** *Let's go windsurfing!*

1 3.47 **Listen and repeat. Then match the phrases in the Vocabulary box to photos a–f in the magazine article.**

Vocabulary Healthy lifestyle

brush your teeth do exercise
drink a lot of water eat fruit and vegetables
go to bed early have friends

1 Photo a: *drink a lot of water*
2 Photo b: ______
3 Photo c: ______
4 Photo d: ______
5 Photo e: ______
6 Photo f: ______

2 **Tell a partner two healthy things that you do.**

3 3.48 **Read and listen to the text. Match headings A–F to tips 1–6.**

A Healthy teeth
B Be sporty
C Sleep well
D People you like
E Healthy food
F Water is great!

4 **Exam Spot** **Read the text again. Complete the sentences with one word.**

1 It's a good idea to *get* up at the same time every day.
2 Healthy teenagers eat fruit and ______ five times a day.
3 Healthy teenagers drink ______, not cola.
4 It's good to brush your ______ after every meal.
5 When you want to be active, you can walk or ______ your bike to school.
6 ______ can help us with our problems.

5 **Read the sentences. Decide if these things are healthy (✔) or not healthy (✘).**

1 I sleep five hours every night, from 1 to 6 o'clock. ✘
2 I never eat vegetables. ☐
3 I often brush my teeth after dinner but never after breakfast. ☐
4 I go swimming at the weekend. ☐
5 I meet my friends two or three times every week. ☐

Teen health

Read our top tips!

1 C A healthy teenager sleeps from ten to six o'clock. Go to bed early and get up at the same time every day! And don't play on your phone for a long time before bed.

2 ☐ Don't say 'I hate vegetables!' Find fruit and vegetables you like and eat them … five times a day! And don't eat a lot of chocolate.

3 ☐ Healthy teenagers drink a lot of water. Have water in your schoolbag, not cola!

4 ☐ How often do you brush your teeth? Just after breakfast? Brush them after every meal every day! You can brush them after lunch at school too!

5 ☐ Do you like football, swimming or volleyball? No? No problem! You can ride your bike to school or walk to be active every day.

6 ☐ Do you play computer games or watch TV after school? Hang out with your friends sometimes. Friends are fun and they help us with our problems.

8.6 Listening and Writing

I can understand and write short texts about healthy lifestyle.

1 **Complete the sentences about sports champions with *train*, *good* and *healthy*.**

a Champions are __________ at their sport.
b They __________ a lot.
c They have got a __________ lifestyle.

2 **3.49 Listen to the interviews with Denise and Gary. What are their sports?**

3 **Exam Spot** **3.49 Listen again. Read the questions and complete the interviewer's notes about Denise and Gary.**

Denise

1 Where does she play volleyball?
At __City__ Club.
2 When does she train?
At ______ o'clock in the morning.
3 How often does she eat fruit and vegetables?
______ day.
4 Has she got time for homework?
______ .

Gary

5 How many friends has Gary got in his club?
He's got ______ friends.
6 When does Gary train?
From five to ______ every day.
7 When are Gary's competitions?
Usually on ______ mornings.
8 What does Gary always eat on Saturdays?
______ .

4 **Have Denise and Gary got a healthy lifestyle? Tell a partner.**

5 **Has Lucas got a healthy lifestyle? Read his blog and find out.**

My lifestyle!

Sleep: I go to bed at half past nine on school days and I get up at eight o'clock. I *love* sleeping!

Food: My favourite food is pizza. Mum and Dad don't like pizza. Yes, really! They like fruit and vegetables … . I drink a lot of water.

Sports and friends: I'm not very sporty but I like watching football on TV. I love music and I play the guitar every day after school from 5 to 6. I often hang out with Jen, Alex and Lian too!

Writing
Checking for grammar mistakes

Read through the first draft of your text to check for grammar mistakes. Check your final draft too.
I love ~~sleep~~ sleeping.

6 **Correct the underlined mistakes.**

1 I like eat chocolate. __*eating*__
2 I hate swimming but my friends like him. ______
3 He eat a healthy breakfast. ______
4 We like do sports. ______

7 **Writing Time** **Write about your lifestyle.**

Find ideas
Make notes under these headings.

Sleep	*I go to bed at … / I get up at …*
Food	*My favourite food is …*
Sports and friends	*I'm / I'm not very sporty.* *I love/like/don't like/ hate …* *I often/sometimes hang out with …*

Draft
Write about your lifestyle.

Check and write
Check your grammar and write the final version of your text.

Language Revision 8.7

Vocabulary

1 Read sentences 1–5. Then complete the words to find the names of sports.

1 You play these sports with a ball.
- a b*asketball*
- b t_______ t_______
- c t_______

2 You don't usually play these sports in a team.
- a r_______ s_______
- b sk_______
- c t_______

3 You do these sports inside and outside.
- a f_______
- b h_______
- c v_______
- d c_______
- e b_______
- f s_______

4 You do these sports in the winter.
- a s_______
- b i_______-s_______

5 You need windy weather for these sports.
- a w_______
- b s_______

2 Jamie's lifestyle isn't healthy. Help him! Complete the sentences with the words in the box.

teeth friends water vegetables ~~Do~~ early

1 *Do* exercise every day.
2 Eat fruit and ________ .
3 Drink a lot of ________.
4 Brush your ________ after you eat.
5 Hang out with your ________.
6 Go to bed ________ .

Grammar

3 Read again about Jamie. Put the verbs in the correct form.

Jamie isn't very sporty. He doesn't like [1] *doing* (do) sports at school and he doesn't like [2]________ (play) football with his friends. He [3]________ (hate) cycling too. He sometimes [4]________ (go) roller skating with his sister. They like [5]________ (go) to the park but not when it's cold and rainy. Jamie loves [6]________ (watch) sports on TV at home!

4 Write questions. Then ask and answer in pairs.

1 sport / your / What's / favourite / ? *What's your favourite sport?*
2 many / sports / you / How / do / train / ? ________________
3 is / Who / teacher / your / ? ________________
4 you / When / train / do / ? ________________
5 do / you / Where / train / ? ________________
6 you / got / a sports hero / Have / ? ________________

5 Read the sentences. Replace the underlined object pronouns with the words in the box.

winter sports	your sister	chocolate	~~your mum~~	Mr Smith

1 I like her. *your mum*
2 I don't like them. __________
3 I love it! __________
4 They like him. __________
5 I can help her. __________

Pronunciation

6 3.50 Listen and repeat: /r/.

Rosemary and Jane
Love running in the rain!

Communication

7 Match the sentence halves 1–4 to a–d.

1 What's the weather
2 It's sunny but it's
3 It's often rainy
4 It's sometimes cold in

a in summer in the UK.
b the UK in the winter.
c windy.
d like in the UK today?

Check yourself! ☑

- I can talk about sports. ☐
- I can use verbs *love/like/don't like/hate + -ing*. ☐
- I can use object pronouns. ☐
- I can ask detailed questions. ☐
- I can talk about the weather. ☐

Reading and Writing

SPORTS WEEK

What sports do you like? What's your favourite sport? Write and tell us!

1 I'm not usually very sporty. I hate team sports and I don't like water sports. But there is one sport I love. It's table tennis! I'm really good at it. It's my favourite.
I play every day at school with my school friends in summer and in winter. I play in school competitions too. I usually win!

Jill, 11

2 I'm in a football club and I play hockey but my favourite sport isn't a ball sport. It's skiing.
There are some great places to ski in my country, Argentina. I always go skiing in August with my family. Yes, August! It's winter here in August.

Rod, 12

3 My best friend's got a boat and I go sailing in the summer. That's cool but my number one sport is swimming.
I go to my town's swimming pool on Mondays and Fridays after school with my swimming club. I don't often swim in the sea. The water is very cold in Scotland!

Alistair, 13

1 Work in pairs. Look at photos A–C. What sports do you use the objects in?

2 Read texts 1–3 and match them to photos A–C.

3 Read the questions and complete the table.

	What's his/her favourite sport?	Where does he/she do it?	Who does he/she do it with?
Jill	*table tennis*		
Rod			
Alistair			

4 **Exam Spot** Complete the text with words in the box. There are two extra words.

My [1] *body* and head are orange and black. I see with my two yellow [2]_____ . My four [3]_____ are very strong. I've got big teeth and I'm dangerous. I can run very fast. I don't eat fruit and [4]_____ . I usually eat meat. I like the [5]_____ but I don't like very hot weather. Do I like [6]_____ ? Yes, I like water! What am I? I am a tiger.

a ~~body~~

b sun

c man

d swimming

e eyes

f vegetables

g teeth

h legs

5 **Exam Spot** Write 40–50 words about your favourite sport. Use these questions to help you.

1 What's your favourite sport?
2 When do you do it?
3 Where do you do it?
4 Who do you do it with?
5 Are you a champion?

My favourite sport is …
I do/go/play … at … / on … / with
I'm / I'm not a champion and/but
I always/sometimes/never win.

Listening

6 **Exam Spot** 3.51 **Listen and match names 1–4 to pictures a–f. There are two extra pictures.**

1 [*e*] Beatrice 2 [ ] Charlie 3 [ ] Mel 4 [ ] Jeff

a

b

c

d

e

f

Communication

7 **Exam Spot** **Read the answers and complete the questions.**

1 A: Have *you got any tickets for the concert*?
B: Yes, we have. There are a lot of tickets.
2 A: Can ______________________?
B: Yes, sure. Three tickets are twenty-seven pounds, please.
3 A: Where ______________________?
B: It's June so the concert is in the park.
4 A: Can ______________________?
B: Yes. You can buy CDs at the concert.
5 A: What time ______________________?
B: At 8 o'clock.

8 **Exam Spot** **Work in pairs. Ask and answer the questions.**

1 What do you do to relax?
2 Where do you go for your holidays?
3 What's the weather like in winter in your country?
4 Have you got an apple in your schoolbag?

Exam Language Bank

Wild animals
bird
butterfly
crocodile
elephant
fish
fly
frog
giraffe
kangaroo
lion
monkey
snake
spider
tiger
whale

Pets
cat
dog
goldfish
hamster
iguana
parrot
rabbit
tortoise

Sports
badminton
basketball
cycling
football
hockey
ice-skating
roller skating
sailing
skateboarding
skiing
swimming
table tennis
taekwondo
tennis
volleyball
windsurfing

Healthy lifestyle
brush your teeth
do exercise
drink a lot of water
eat fruit and vegetables
go to bed early
have friends

Adjectives
cute	fast	strong
dangerous	slow	ugly

Buying a ticket
Can I help you?
Can I have *a ticket/two tickets to the zoo*, please?
That's *eighteen pounds fifty*.
Here you are.
Here is your ticket. / Here are are your tickets.
Thanks.

Talking about the weather
What's the weather like?
It's *cloudy/cold/hot/rainy/snowy/ sunny/warm/ windy*.
It's *cold/hot/rainy/sunny* in *winter/summer/ autumn/spring*.

Answers

Unit 0 Lesson 0.3, Page 9, Exercise 6

1

2
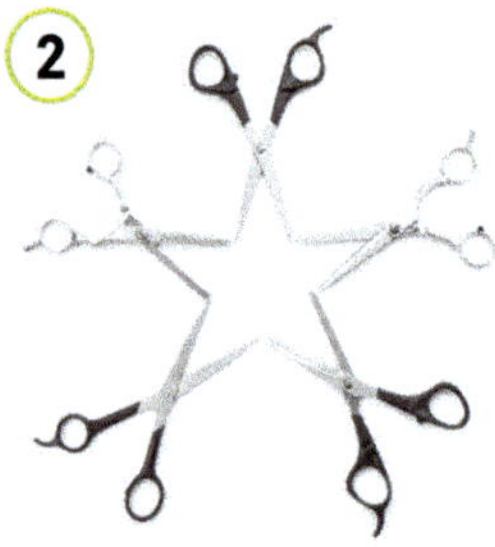

3

4

5
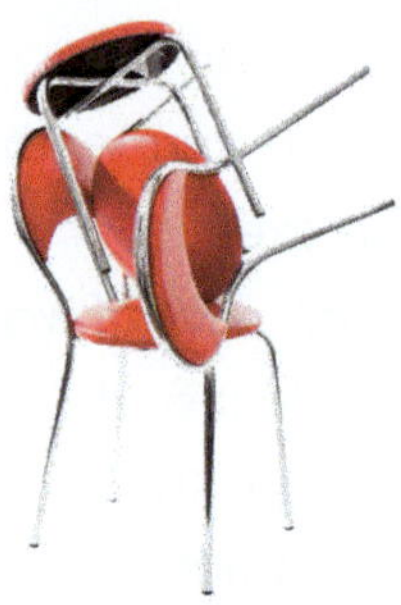

6
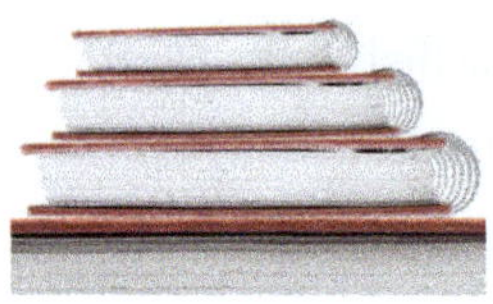

Unit 5 Lesson 5.5, Page 65, Exercise 4

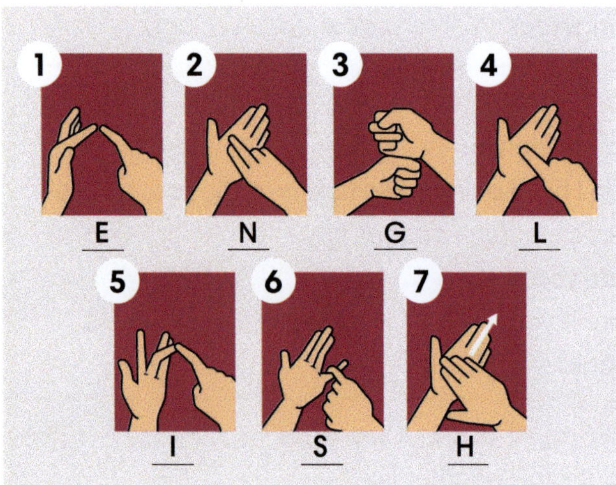

Student A activities

Unit 1 Lesson 1.5, Page 17, exercise 7

Describe the photos. Use the example to help you.

A: *'It's mum, dad, and three sons. They are on holiday'.*

B: *It's photo A.*

A

B

C

D

Unit 7 Lesson 7.2, page 85, Exercise 10

4 Granny wants to go for walks with her pet.
5 Aunt Megan loves birds.
6 Emma doesn't want a big pet.

Songs and raps

Unit 0 Lesson 0.1, Page 5, Exercise 4

1.3 1.4 **Alphabet Rap**

, , , D,

E, F, G,

Say the alphabet, say it with me!

H, I, J, K, L, M, N, O, P,

 is funny as you can see.

R, S, T, U and V

four more letters and we're free.

W, X, Y and

Shh …  is sleepy, so are we!

Unit 2 Lesson 2.3, Page 27, Exercise 9

1.42 1.43 **Kit's Rap**

Is she clever? Yes, she is.
Is she fun? She's all that!
Is she the best? Her name's Kit
Is she the one? and she's a cool cat!

Now you rap. You can rap about a friend!

Unit 5 Lesson 5.3, Page 63, Exercise 9

2.42 2.43 **Activities Rap**

I can act, I can sing, I can draw a cat
I can dive, I can swim – Can you do all that?
I can act, I can sing, I can draw a cat.
I can dive, I can swim – I can do all that!

Now you rap. Use different activities you know.

Unit 7 Lesson 7.3, Page 87, Exercise 10

3.24 3.25 **Questions Song**

Do you play computer games?
Do you watch TV?
Do you hang out with your friends?
Then you're just like me!
Yes, you're just like me!

Does your mum say 'Get up now!'?
Does she count to three?
Do you say 'Oh, it's not fair!'?
Then you're just like me!
Yes, you're just like me!

Do you have your breakfast?
Do you go to school?
Do you like your English class?
Then you're really cool!
Yes, you're really cool!

Unit 4 Lesson 4.3, Page 51, Exercise 9

2.23 2.24 **Robots' Song**

Have you got super ears,
Have you got super eyes?

Yes, we've got superpowers,
We are super guys!

Have you got super arms,
or maybe a super nose?

We have got super feet
And twenty super toes!

Have you got a super boat,
Have you got a bike?

No, we've got a super car,
And its name is Mike!

Pairwork activities

Unit 3 Lesson 3.2, Page 37, Exercise 11

Play a drawing dictation game. Describe one of the pictures for your partner to draw.

1

2

3

4

Unit 3 Lesson 3.3, Page 39, Exercise 7

Play a memory game.
Student A: Choose one of the pictures above.
Close your book.
Student B: Ask Student A questions.
Then swap roles.

A: *Picture 1.*
B: *Chairs?*
A: *There are four chairs.*

Student B activities

Unit 1 Lesson 1.5, Page 17, exercise 7

Describe the photos. Use the example to help you.

A: *'It's mum, dad, and three sons. They are on holiday'.*
B: *It's photo A.*

A

B

C

D

Unit 7 Lesson 7.2, page 85, Exercise 10

1 Alex wants to play with his pet.
2 Lucas doesn't like birds.
3 Lian's mum is allergic to cats and rabbits.

Unit 0
Get started!

Vocabulary
Numbers 1–20
1 one /wʌn/
2 two /tuː/
3 three /θriː/
4 four /fɔː/
5 five /faɪv/
6 six /sɪks/
7 seven /'sevən/
8 eight /eɪt/
9 nine /naɪn/
10 ten /ten/
11 eleven /ɪ'levən/
12 twelve /twelv/
13 thirteen /ˌθɜː'tiːn/
14 fourteen /ˌfɔː'tiːn/
15 fifteen /ˌfɪf'tiːn/
16 sixteen /ˌsɪk'stiːn/
17 seventeen /ˌsevən'tiːn/
18 eighteen /ˌeɪ'tiːn/
19 nineteen /ˌnaɪn'tiːn/
20 twenty /'twenti/

Numbers 10–100
10 ten /ten/
20 twenty /'twenti/
30 thirty /'θɜːti/
40 forty /'fɔːti/
50 fifty /'fɪfti/
60 sixty /'sɪksti/
70 seventy /'seventi/
80 eighty /'eɪti/
90 ninety /'naɪnti/
100 a hundred /ə 'hʌndrəd/

Colours
black /blæk/
blue /bluː/
brown /braʊn/
green /griːn/
grey /greɪ/
orange /'ɒrəndʒ/
pink /pɪŋk/
purple /'pɜːpəl/
red /red/
white /waɪt/
yellow /'jeləʊ/

In my bag
book /bʊk/
coloured pencil /ˌkʌləd 'pensəl/
notebook /'nəʊtbʊk/
pen /pen/
pencil /'pensəl/
pencil case /'pensəl keɪs/
pencil sharpener /'pensəl ʃɑːpənə/
rubber /'rʌbə/
ruler /'ruːlə/
sandwich /'sæn(d)wɪdʒ/
scissors /'sɪzəz/

Classroom objects
bin /bɪn/
board /bɔːd/
chair /tʃeə/
clock /klɒk/
desk /desk/

Classroom language
Close your books.
Listen *(to the story)*.
Look *(at the photo)*.
Open your books.
Read *(the text)*.
Sit down.
Stand up.
Work in pairs.
Write *(your name)*, please.
***
Can you help me?
Can you repeat (that)?
I'm ready.
What's *kredka* in English?

Other
cupcake /'kʌpkeɪk/
double /'dʌbəl/

Unit 1
Family and friends

1.1

Vocabulary Family
aunt /ɑːnt/
brother /'brʌðə/
cousin /'kʌzən/
dad /dæd/
daughter /'dɔːtə/
father /'fɑːðə/
grandfather/grandad /'grændˌfɑːðə/'grændæd/
grandmother/granny /'grænˌmʌðə/'græni/
mother /'mʌðə/
mum /mʌm/
parents /'peərənts/
sister /'sɪstə/
son /sʌn/
uncle /'ʌŋkəl/

1.2

Say it!
Be careful! /ˌbi 'keəfəl/
Hold this, please! /'həʊld ðɪs ˌpliːz/
I've got it! /ˌaɪv 'gɒt ɪt/

Other
best friend /ˌbest 'frend/
birthday /'bɜːθdeɪ/
birthday cake /'bɜːθdeɪ keɪk/
card /kɑːd/
class /klɑːs/
classmate /'klɑːsmeɪt/
eat /iːt/
friend /frend/
from /frɒm/
happy /'hæpi/
Happy birthday! /ˌhæpi 'bɜːθdeɪ/
Let's have a break. /lets v eɪ breɪk/
lovely /'lʌvli/
my darling /ˌmaɪ 'dɑːlɪŋ/
present /'prezənt/
school trip /'skuːl trɪp/
She is 70 years old. /ʃi ɪz ˌseventi ˌjɪəz 'əʊld/
The cake is a mess. /ðə keɪk s eɪ mes/
We're ready for the cake. /wɪə 'redi fə ðə keɪk/
yummy /'jʌmi/

1.3

Vocabulary Countries and nationalities
American /ə'merəkən/
British /'brɪtɪʃ/
China /'tʃaɪn ə/
Chinese /ˌtʃaɪ'niːz/
France /frɑːns/
French /frentʃ/
Italian /ɪ'tæliən/
Italy /'ɪtəli/
Poland /'pəʊlənd/
Polish /'pəʊlɪʃ/
Spain /speɪn/
Spanish /'spænɪʃ/
the UK /ðə ˌjuː 'keɪ /
the USA /ðə ˌjuː es 'eɪ/

Other
Bye now! /'baɪ naʊ/
family album /'fæməli ˌælbəm/
Help! /help/
hungry /'hʌŋgri/
in the photo /ɪn ðə 'fəʊtəʊ/
name /neɪm/
No idea. /ˌnəʊ aɪ'dɪə/
Sorry. /'sɒri/
superhero /'suːpəˌhɪərəʊ/
What about you? /wɒt ə'baʊt jə/
You're right. /ˌjɔː 'raɪt/

1.4

Communication Introductions
He is my classmate.
He is my friend.
Hello, Lucas.
Lucas, this is my mum.
Mum, this is Lucas.
Nice to meet you.
Nice to meet you too.

Other
bag /bæg/
famous /'feɪməs/
film star /fɪlm stɑː/
kids /kɪdz/
Let's go. /ˌlets 'gəʊ/
neighbour /'neɪbə/
pop star /pɒp stɑː/
sports person /spɔːts 'pɜːsən/

1.5

Vocabulary Places
at a party /ət ə 'pɑːti/
at home /ət 'həʊm/
at school /ət 'skuːl/
in the garden /ɪn ðə 'gɑːdn/
in the park /ɪn ðə 'pɑːk/
on holiday /ɒn 'hɒlədeɪ/

Other
favourite /'feɪvərət/
great /greɪt/
I'm four. /ˌaɪm 'fɔː/
near /nɪə/
She's fun! /ˌʃiz 'fʌn/
too /tuː/

1.6

Other
interesting /'ɪntrəstɪŋ/
International Friendship Day /ɪntəˌnæʃənəl 'frendʃɪp deɪ/
spell /spel/

Get Culture
English around the world
biggest /'bɪg ɪst/
capital city /'kæpətl 'sɪti/
different /'dɪfərənt/
flag /flæg/
live /lɪv/
most people /məʊst 'piːpəl/
speak /spiːk/
summer /'sʌmə/
winter /'wɪntə/

Unit 2
My things

2.1

Vocabulary Clothes
boots /buːts/
cap /kæp/
coat /kəʊt/
dress /dres/
hoodie /'hʊdi/
jacket /'dʒækət/
jeans /dʒiːnz/
jumper /'dʒʌmpə/
shirt /ʃɜːt/
shoes /ʃuːz/
skirt /skɜːt/
T-shirt /'tiː ʃɜːt/
top /tɒp/
tracksuit /'træksuːt/
trainers /'treɪnəz/
trousers /'traʊzəz/

Other
at the weekend /ət ðə ˌwiːk'end, 'wiːkend/

2.2

Vocabulary Adjectives
big /bɪg/
boring /'bɔːrɪŋ/
cool /kuːl/
long /lɒŋ/
new /njuː/
old /əʊld/
short /ʃɔːt/
small /smɔːl/

Word list

Say it!
Hang on! /ˌhæŋ 'ɒn/
Here you are. /'hɪə jə ˌɑː/
Over there. /ˌəʊvə 'ðeə/
What's up? /ˌwɒts 'ʌp/

Other
put away /ˌpʊt ə'weɪ/
too (small) /tuː (smɔːl)/

2.3

Other
Are you sure? /ˌɑː jə 'ʃɔː/
box /bɒks/
boy /bɔɪ/
clever cat /'klevə 'kæt/
cool /ˌkuːl/
girl /gɜːl/
size /saɪz/
suit /suːt/

2.4

Communication
Asking for personal information
How old are you?
What's your favourite film?
What's your favourite music?
What's your favourite sport?
What's your name?
Where are you from?
Who's your favourite actor?
Who's your favourite singer?
Who's your favourite sports person?

Other
Good question. /gʊd 'kwestʃ(ə)n/
High five! /ˌhaɪ 'faɪv/
rock /rɒk/
school band /ˌskuːl 'bænd/

2.5

Vocabulary My things
backpack /'bækpæk/
games console /'geɪmz kənˌsəʊl/
laptop computer /ˌlæptɒp kəm'pjuːtə/
mobile phone /ˌməʊbaɪl 'fəʊn/
mountain bike /'maʊntən baɪk/
skateboard /'skeɪtbɔːd/

Other
Congratulations! /kənˌgrætʃə'leɪʃənz/
Don't worry! /ˌdəʊnt 'wʌri/
even /'iːvən/
fantastic /fæn'tæstɪk/
favourites /'feɪvrəts/
gadget /'gædʒət/
How cool is that? /haʊ ˌkuːl ɪz 'ðæt/
No problem. /ˌnəʊ 'prɒbləm/
pet /pet/
pocket /'pɒkət/
right size /raɪt saɪz/
That's easy. /ðæts 'iːzi/
That's not all. /ˌðæts nɒt 'ɔːl/
That's right. /ˌðæts 'raɪt/
You're cold. /ˌjɔː 'kəʊld/

Unit 3
In the house

3.1

Vocabulary In the house
Parts of the house
bathroom /'bɑːθrʊm/
bedroom /'bedrʊm/
door /dɔː/
floor /flɔː/
garage /'gærɪdʒ/
garden /'gɑːdn/
kitchen /'kɪtʃən/
living room /'lɪvɪŋ ruːm/
wall /wɔːl/
window /'wɪndəʊ/

Inside the house
armchair /'ɑːmtʃeə/
bath /bɑːθ/
bed /bed/
chair /tʃeə/
desk /desk/
fridge /frɪdʒ/
sofa /'səʊfə/
table /'teɪbəl/
wardrobe /'wɔːdrəʊb/

3.2

Vocabulary
Prepositions of place
behind /bɪ'haɪnd/
in /ɪn/
in front of /ɪn 'frʌnt əv/
next to /'nekst tə/
on /ɒn/
under /'ʌndə/

Say it!
Right there! /ˌraɪt 'ðeə/
There it is! /'ðeər ɪt ɪz/
Wait! /weɪt/
Yuk! /jʌk/

Other
carton /'kɑːtn/
DVD /ˌdiː viː 'diː/
maybe /'meɪbi/
milk /mɪlk/
orange juice /'ɒrəndʒ dʒuːs/
some /səm/
sweets /swiːts/

3.3

Other
bad people /ˌbæd 'piːpəl/
car /kɑː/
go /gəʊ/
naughty /'nɔːti/
number /'nʌmbə/
parrot /'pærət/
silly /'sɪli/
tree /triː/

3.4

Communication
Having a guest
Hello.
It's downstairs.
It's next to the living room.
It's upstairs.
Let me show you.
No, thank you.
Please, come in.
Thank you.
Where's the bathroom, please?
Would you like a sandwich?
Yes, please.

Other
another /ə'nʌðə(r)/
I'd like … /ˌaɪd 'laɪk/
Not really. /ˌnɒt 'rɪəli/

3.5

Vocabulary
Household objects
carpet /'kɑːpət/
cushion /'kʊʃən/
lamp /læmp/
plant /plɑːnt/
poster /'pəʊstə/
television (TV) /'teləˌvɪʒən (ˌtiː 'viː)/

Other
competition /ˌkɒmpə'tɪʃən/
dream /driːm/
inside /ɪn'saɪd/
It looks typical. /ɪt ˌlʊks 'tɪpɪkəl/
look at /'lʊk ət/
perfect /'pɜːfɪkt/
picture /'pɪktʃə/
skateboarder /'skeɪtbɔːdə/
something /'sʌmθɪŋ/
Think about it! /'θɪŋk əˌbaʊt ɪt/
train /treɪn/
Why? /waɪ/

Get Culture
Houses in the UK

Types of houses
block of flats /blɒk əv flæts/
cottage /'kɒtɪdʒ/
detached house /dɪ'tætʃt haʊs/
houseboat /'haʊsbəʊt/
semi-detached house /'semi dɪ'tætʃt haʊs/
terraced houses /'terəst 'haʊz ɪz/

Other
country /'kʌntri/
fantastic /fæn'tæstɪk/
floor /flɔː/
next door /nekst dɔː/
tree-house /triː haʊs/
view /vjuː/

Unit 4
About me

4.1

Vocabulary
Face and hair
Face
ears /ɪəz/
eyes /aɪz/
mouth /maʊθ/
nose /nəʊz/
teeth /tiːθ/

Hair
blond /blɒnd/
curly /'kɜːli/
dark /dɑːk/
red /red/
spiky /'spaɪki/
straight /streɪt/
wavy /'weɪvi/

4.2

Vocabulary
Parts of the body
arm /ɑːm/
body /'bɒdi/
fingers /'fɪŋgəz/
foot /fʊt/
hand /hænd/
head /hed/
leg /leg/
neck /nek/
toes /təʊz/

Say it!
Help me, please! /'help mi pliːz/
It isn't my fault! /ɪt ˌɪzənt maɪ 'fɔːlt/
Stop it! /'stɒp ɪt/

Other
a lot of /ə 'lɒt əv/
fine /faɪn/
high /haɪ/
Hurry up! /ˌhʌri 'ʌp/
Ouch! /aʊtʃ/
tall /tɔːl/
time /taɪm/

4.3

Other
battery power /'bætəri ˌpaʊə/
hero /'hɪərəʊ/
like /laɪk/
super power /'suːpə ˌpaʊə/

4.4

Communication
Apologising
Are you OK?
I'm so sorry.
Sorry about that!
Sorry, my mistake.
* * *
I'm fine.
It's OK.
No problem.
That's all right.

Other
house keys /haʊs ki:z/
Oh, dear. /əʊ dɪə/
sweetie /'swi:ti/

4.5

Vocabulary
Personality adjectives
clever /'klevə/
friendly /'frendli/
funny /'fʌni/
helpful /'helpfəl/
nice /naɪs/
sporty /'spɔ:ti/
Other
always /'ɔ:lwəz/
answer /'ɑ:nsə/
dancing /'dɑ:nsɪŋ/
do a quiz /ˌdu: ə 'kwɪz/
good at /'gʊd ət/
good student /ˌgʊd 'stju:dənt/
group /gru:p/
hobby /'hɒbi/
home lover /'həʊm ˌlʌvə/
homework /'həʊmwɜ:k/
How many? /ˌhaʊ 'meni/
joke /dʒəʊk/
kind /kaɪnd/
party animal /ˌpɑ:ti 'ænəməl/
person /'pɜ:sən/
personality /ˌpɜ:sə'næləti/
place /pleɪs/
reading /'ri:dɪŋ/
room /ru:m/
say /seɪ/
sometimes /'sʌmtaɪmz/
speak to /'spi:k tə/
subject /'sʌbdʒɪkt/
usually /'ju:ʒuəli/

Unit 5
Things I can do

5.1

Vocabulary
Action verbs
act /ækt/
climb /klaɪm/
cook /kʊk/
dive /daɪv/
draw /drɔ:/
fix /fɪks/
fly /flaɪ/
jump /dʒʌmp/
read /ri:d/
ride /raɪd/
run /rʌn/
sing /sɪŋ/
skateboard /'skeɪtbɔ:d/
swim /swɪm/
write /raɪt/

5.2

Vocabulary
make, play, ride
make a poster /ˌmeɪk ə 'pəʊstə/
make cupcakes /ˌmeɪk 'kʌpkeɪks/
play computer games /ˌpleɪ kəm'pju:tə geɪmz/
play football /ˌpleɪ 'fʊtbɔ:l/
play the piano /ˌpleɪ ðə pi'ænəʊ/
ride a bike /ˌraɪd ə 'baɪk/
ride a horse /ˌraɪd ə 'hɔ:s/
Say it!
Let me see … /ˌlet mi 'si:/
Not again! /ˌnɒt ə'gen/
What's wrong? /ˌwɒts 'rɒŋ/
Other
all day /ˌɔ:l 'deɪ/
camera /'kæmərə/
can /kæn/
I can't see a thing. /aɪ ˌkɑ:nt ˌsi: ə 'θɪŋ/
talented /'tæləntəd/
video /'vɪdiəʊ/
well /wel/

5.3

Other
boat /bəʊt/
fast /fɑ:st/
lovely day /ˌlʌvli 'deɪ/
One minute, please. /ˌwʌn 'mɪnət ˌpli:z/
who /hu:/

5.4

Communication
Suggestions
Let's do something fun!
Let's go ice skating!
We can go to the park!
* * *
Great idea!
I agree!
I'm not sure.
It's not a good idea.
Let's do that!
Other
guys /gaɪz/
teach /ti:tʃ/
wear /weə/

5.5

Other
alphabet /'ælfəbet/
course /kɔ:s/
hear /hɪə/
important /ɪm'pɔ:tənt/
language /'læŋgwɪdʒ/
learn /lɜ:n/
letter /'letə/
make friends with /ˌmeɪk 'frendz wɪð/
sign language /'saɪn ˌlæŋgwɪdʒ/
teacher /'ti:tʃə/
TV programme /ˌti: 'vi: ˌprəʊgræm/
word /wɜ:d/

5.6

Other
after school /ˌɑ:ftə 'sku:l/
ball /bɔ:l/
class /klɑ:s/
club /klʌb/
come /kʌm/
game /geɪm/
now /naʊ/
paint /peɪnt/
star /stɑ:/
today /tə'deɪ/

Get Culture
Kid's London
activity /æk'tɪvəti, æk'tɪvɪti/
comic /'kɒmɪk/
dinosaur /'daɪnəsɔ:/
from the top of /frəm ðə tɒp əv/
kid /kɪd/
museum /mju:'ziəm/
musical /'mju:zɪkəl/
puppet /'pʌpət, 'pʌpɪt/
scientist /'saɪəntəst, 'saɪəntɪst/
show /ʃəʊ/
together /tə'geðə/
workshop /'wɜ:kʃɒp/

Unit 6
My day

6.1

Vocabulary
Daily activities
do my homework /ˌdu: maɪ 'həʊmwɜ:k/
get up /ˌget 'ʌp/
go to bed /ˌgəʊ tə 'bed/
go to school /ˌgəʊ tə 'sku:l/
hang out with my friends / hæŋ ˌaʊt wɪð maɪ 'frendz/
have a shower /ˌhæv ə 'ʃaʊə/
have breakfast /ˌhæv 'brekfəst/
have dinner /ˌhæv 'dɪnə/
have lessons /ˌhæv 'lesənz/
have lunch /ˌhæv 'lʌntʃ/
listen to music /ˌlɪsən tə 'mju:zɪk/
tidy my room /ˌtaɪdi maɪ 'ru:m/
watch TV /ˌwɒtʃ ˌti: 'vi:/

6.2

Say it!
Come on, guys! /ˌkʌm 'ɒn gaɪz/
Me too. /ˌmi 'tu:/
Seriously? /'sɪəriəsli/
Other
classical music /ˌklæsɪkəl 'mju:zɪk/
daily routine /'deɪli ru:'ti:n/
early /'ɜ:li/
get ready for school /get ˌredi fə 'sku:l/
in the evening /ˌɪn ði 'i:vnɪŋ/
late for school /ˌleɪt fə 'sku:l/
never /'nevə/
pancakes /'pænkeɪks/
really /'rɪəli/
school survey /sku:l 'sɜ:veɪ/
walk /wɔ:k/

6.3

Vocabulary
Days of the week
Monday /'mʌndi/
Tuesday /'tju:zdi/
Wednesday /'wenzdi/
Thursday /'θɜ:zdi/
Friday /'fraɪdi/
Saturday /'sætədi/
Sunday /'sʌndi/
Other
busy /'bɪzi/
busy week /ˌbɪzi 'wi:k/
free day /ˌfri: 'deɪ/
gym /dʒɪm/
How about Tuesday? /ˌhaʊ əˌbaʊt 'tju:zdi/
mess /mes/
often /'ɒfən/
swimming lesson /'swɪmɪŋ ˌlesən/
team /ti:m/
visit /'vɪzət/

6.4

Communication
Telling the time
What time is it?
It's four o'clock.
* * *
What time is the film?
What time is the match?
It's at ten (minutes) past four.
It's at quarter past four.
It's at half past four.
It's at quarter to five.
It's at ten (minutes) to five.
Other
That's better. /ˌðæts 'betə/
The film is on again at … / ðə fɪlm s ɒn ə'gen ət/
too late /ˌtu: 'leɪt/

6.5

Vocabulary Months
January /'dʒænjuəri/
February /'februəri/
March /mɑ:tʃ/
April /'eɪprəl/
May /meɪ/
June /dʒu:n/
July /dʒʊ'laɪ/
August /'ɔ:gəst/
September /sep'tembə/
October /ɒk'təʊbə/

Word list

November /nəʊ'vembə/
December /dɪ'sembə/

Other

animal /'ænɪm(ə)l/
blog /blɒg/
every /'evri/
life /laɪf/
live /lɪv/
love /lʌv/
my own /maɪ əʊn/
online /'ɒnlaɪn/
teenagers /'tiːnˌeɪdʒə(r)z/
travel /'træv(ə)l/
walking /'wɔːkɪŋ/
writing /'raɪtɪŋ/

6.6

Other

grandparents /'grændˌpeərənts/
meet my friend /ˌmiːt maɪ 'frend/
take the bus /ˌteɪk ðə 'bʌs/

Unit 7

Animals

7.1

Vocabulary
Wild animals

bird /bɜːd/
butterfly /'bʌtəflaɪ/
crocodile /'krɒkədaɪl/
elephant /'eləfənt/
fish /fɪʃ/
fly /flaɪ/
frog /frɒg/
giraffe /dʒə'rɑːf/
kangaroo /ˌkæŋgə'ruː/
lion /'laɪən/
monkey /'mʌŋki/
snake /sneɪk/
spider /'spaɪdə/
tiger /'taɪgə/
whale /weɪl/

7.2

Vocabulary Pets

cat /kæt/
dog /dɒg/
goldfish /'gəʊldˌfɪʃ/
hamster /'hæmstə/
iguana /ɪ'gwɑːnə/
parrot /'pærət/
rabbit /'ræbət/
tortoise /'tɔːtəs/

Say it!

I don't mind! /aɪ ˌdəʊnt 'maɪnd/
Oh, all right! /əʊ ˌɔːl 'raɪt/
Poor (dog)! /ˌpɔː ('dɒg)/

Other

at the weekend /ət ðəˌwiːk'end/
because /bɪ'kɒz/
before /bɪ'fɔː/
every day /ˌevri 'deɪ/
hard work /ˌhɑːd 'wɜːk/
I'm allergic (to) /aɪm əˌlɜːdʒɪk (tə)/
puppy /'pʌpi/
take the dog for a walk /ˌteɪk ðə ˌdɒg fər ə 'wɔːk/

7.3

Other

at all /ət 'ɔːl/
foreign language /ˌfɒrən 'læŋgwɪdʒ/
interview /'ɪntəvjuː/
magazine /ˌmægə'ziːn/
player /'pleɪə/
relax /rɪ'læks/
reporter /rɪ'pɔːtə/
together /tə'geðə/
win /wɪn/
work /wɜːk/

7.4

Communication
Buying a ticket

Can I have one ticket to the zoo, please?
Can I have two tickets to the zoo, please?
Can I help you?
Here are your tickets.
Here is your ticket.
Here you are.
Thanks.
That's eighteen pounds fifty.

Other

guide /'gaɪd/
I could eat a horse. /aɪ kəd iːt eɪ hɔːs/
pass /pɑːs/
start /stɑːt/

7.5

Vocabulary
Adjectives

cute /kjuːt/
dangerous /'deɪndʒərəs/
fast /fɑːst/
slow /sləʊ/
strong /strɒŋ/
ugly /'ʌgli/

Other

amazing /ə'meɪzɪŋ/
at 55 kilometres an hour /ət ˌfɪfti ˌfaɪv ˌkɪləmiːtəz ən 'aʊə/
drink /drɪŋk/
food /fuːd/
having fun /ˌhævɪŋ 'fʌn/
hour /aʊə/
jump out /ˌdʒʌmp 'aʊt/
kilo /'kiːləʊ/
leaves /liːvz/
litre /'liːtə/
night /naɪt/
plants /plɑːnts/
sleep /sliːp/
think /θɪŋk/
water /'wɔːtə/

7.6

Other

at night /ət 'naɪt/
children /'tʃɪldrən/
dog food /'dɒg fuːd/
easy /'iːzi/
in the day /ɪn ðə 'deɪ/
it's cold /ˌɪts 'kəʊld/
look after a pet /ˌlʊk ˌɑːftər ə 'pet/
number one /ˌnʌmbə 'wʌn/
pet shop /'pet ʃɒp/
play /pleɪ/

Get Culture
Pets in the UK

exotic /ɪg'zɒtɪk/
lose /luːz/
need /niːd/
quiet /'kwaɪət/
scary /'skeəri/
space /speɪs/
unusual /ʌn'juːʒuəl, -ʒəl/

Unit 8

I like that!

8.1

Vocabulary Sports

badminton /'bædmɪntən/
basketball /'bɑːskətbɔːl/
cycling /'saɪklɪŋ/
football /'fʊtbɔːl/
hockey /'hɒki/
ice-skating /'aɪs ˌskeɪtɪŋ/
roller skating /'rəʊlə ˌskeɪtɪŋ/
sailing /'seɪlɪŋ/
skateboarding /'skeɪtbɔːdɪŋ/
skiing /'skiːɪŋ/
swimming /'swɪmɪŋ/
table tennis /'teɪbəl ˌtenəs/
taekwondo /taɪ'kwɒndəʊ/
tennis /'tenəs/
volleyball /'vɒlibɔːl/
windsurfing /'wɪnd sɜːfɪŋ/

8.2

Say it!

Maybe. /'meɪbi/
That's true. /ˌðæts 'truː/

Other

find /faɪnd/
for example /fər ɪg'zɑːmpəl/
get wet /ˌget 'wet/
hate /heɪt/
horse-riding /'hɔːs ˌraɪdɪŋ/
rock climbing /'rɒk ˌklaɪmɪŋ/
summer camp /ˌsʌmə 'kæmp/
want /wɒnt/
water sports /'wɔːtə spɔːts/

8.3

Other

autograph /'ɔːtəgrɑːf/
fan /fæn/
right now /ˌraɪt 'naʊ/
the same /ðə 'seɪm/
Well done! /ˌwel 'dʌn/
whose /huːz/

8.4

Communication
Talking about the weather

What's the weather like?
It's cloudy.
It's cold.
It's hot.
It's rainy.
It's snowy.
It's sunny.
It's warm.
It's windy.

* * *

It's cold in winter.
It's hot in summer.
It's rainy in autumn.
It's sunny in spring.

Other

appointment /ə'pɔɪntmənt/
at the beach /ət ðə 'biːtʃ/
I hope … /ˌaɪ 'həʊp/
That's a pity. /ˌðæts ə 'pɪti/

8.5

Vocabulary
Healthy lifestyle

brush your teeth /ˌbrʌʃ jə 'tiːθ/
do exercise /ˌduː 'eksəsaɪz/
drink a lot of water /ˌdrɪŋk ə lɒt əv 'wɔːtə/
eat fruit and vegetables /ˌiːt ˌfruːt ənd 'vedʒtəbəlz/
go to bed early /ˌgəʊ tə ˌbed 'ɜːli/
have friends /ˌhæv 'frendz/

Other

active /'æktɪv/
chocolate /'tʃɒklət/
five times a day /ˌfaɪv ˌtaɪmz ə 'deɪ/
for a long time /fər ə ˌlɒŋ 'taɪm/
from … to … /frɒm … tuː …/
health /helθ/
healthy /'helθi/
meal /miːl/
school bag /'skuːlbæg/
tip /tɪp/

8.6

Other

champion /'tʃæmpiən/
competitions /ˌkɒmpə 'tɪʃ ənz/
in the morning /ɪn ðə 'mɔːnɪŋ/
pizza /'piːtsə/